# The Part-Time

# VEGAN

## 201 YUMMY RECIPES That Put the Fun in Flexitarian

### Cherise Grifoni

**Avon, Massachusetts**

Published by
Adams Media, a division of F+W Media, Inc.
57 Littlefield Street, Avon, MA 02322. U.S.A.
*www.adamsmedia.com*

Contains a limited number of recipes previously published in *The Everything® Vegan Cookbook* by Jolinda Hackett with Lorena Novack Bull, RD, copyright © 2010 by F+W Media, Inc., ISBN 10: 1-4405-0216-1, ISBN 13: 978-14405-0216-3.

ISBN 10: 1-4405-1226-4
ISBN 13: 978-1-4405-1226-1
eISBN 10: 1-4405-2505-6
eISBN 13: 978-1-4405-2505-6

Printed in the United States of America.

10 9 8 7 6 5 4 3 2 1

**Library of Congress Cataloging-in-Publication Data**
is available from the publisher.

*This book is available at quantity discounts for bulk purchases.*
*For information, please call 1-800-289-0963.*

## Dedication

For Nadine, and Megan, and David
The world, wind; but never once
have you left me off-balance.
Thank you for that
one
solid truth.

# Acknowledgments

A kiss for mother, Sandy, who is quite actually an angel. You have shown me nothing but kindness throughout my whole life. You are the person who does not judge. You are an anomaly among the human race. You exist in a pool of light. How I have ever deserved you, I cannot say. Other people may think they know what good can be, but they need only look to you.

A salute to father, Jim, because he has taught me the most important lesson that I have ever learned: be tough, or you will break; no one will ever, ever put you back together but yourself.

Thank you to my wonderful and enthusiastic editor, Wendy, without whom this book would not have been possible at all. She is a kind, passionate woman, and she always responded so promptly to my (inevitably) frantic e-mails.

Thank you to my Nunna and Papa, and Papa G, whom I love and who inspire me with their love and their lives.

Thank you to Jared, who helped when he didn't have to. Thank you to Jenn, for believing in me from the start. Thank you to Tammi Kibler of TammiKibler.com for opening these doors. Thank you to Kara, Meredith, Nina, Melissa, Angel, and Maddie for all the good times.

# Table of Contentments

# Totally Not Boring Intro

Let's just get this out there. I'm not here to tell you how to save the world, maybe just how to save your waistline (and your coronary arteries). Shallow? Not a lick. Delicious? Yes, indeed.

Here's the deal: You're curious about veganism but you don't want to read some eco-policing loony drone on and on about how trees are our friends and chickens would rather be playing poker in their hen houses than lay eggs for us. I get it. It doesn't matter if you're a saint; if you're hungry, you're never going to get anything done.

That's where I come in: your no-nonsense, quick-witted guide to veganism. Like neighbors who throw a Christmas party but really wish they weren't doing so, I just want to feed you and be done with it. No ramblings about my vacation to the Andes to save misled alpacas and self-sacrificing do-goodedness that will make you feel like you have just stepped out from the ninth-circle. I just like to eat well.

While I'm not going to bore you with stories you don't want to hear, I do promise to tip you off with the occasional factoid on vegan living that you can add to your ingenious repertoire when you need to outwit your non-vegan friends. Use these as your ammo when they inevitably harangue you about your stellar physique and excellent culinary taste.

Why do we cook with animal milk and eggs? Eggs are usually just binders in recipes, and vegetarian milks can be just as tasty and rich. It's all a matter of experimentation and shaking up what you thought you knew.

Are you curious about where the hell vegans get their protein? What can you possibly eat that doesn't have milk in it?! Won't it taste horrible? Don't vegans only eat spinach and weeds?

Well, kids, here's some news for you.

You *can* have your cake and eat it too. And your ice cream. And your cheesy flavor. You *can* eat honey; you *can* have sugar. All you need are some conscious shopper skills and the right, quick, go-to information.

There are a lot of great sociopolitical, not to mention cruelty-free, reasons to become a vegan. But at the same time, sometimes you just want to do something for *yourself*, am I right? Once you start feeling spectacular and energetic, clean and healthy, and downright *good* about the fresh, colorful, and impressive things that you're eating, you can thank me.

(No, seriously, you're going to want to.)

# CHAPTER 1

# Veganism 101

Veganism is the exclusion of all animal and animal-based products from your diet. This includes meat, eggs, dairy, and gelatin, and it can even extend to some types of sugar and honey.

Fear not, faithful readers. There is always a delicious vegan way around these things.

Perhaps you're finding yourself in a small predicament: you wish to turn (part-time) vegan, but you have nowhere to turn. Maybe you have questions like these:

1. How do you start?
2. What ingredients do you start looking for?
3. And how the hell do you find them?

No worries. You don't need to take a transcontinental ship in order to scout out the new ingredients that will make your transition to veganism both easy and fun. That's what I'm here for!

Now granted, occasionally some vegans get a little weird. There are some recipes out there that include Irish Moss, seaweed, algae, and even brains. Just kidding about the last part, but we're still talking about some unorthodox choices.

Thankfully, all of the recipes in this book will make use of your classic favorite ingredients, some soon-to-be new friends, and fresh, squeaky produce that will help your skin and hair and eyes look bright and beautiful.

## How Do You Start?

When I first became a vegetarian many years ago, I stopped eating meat cold turkey. I was never a big meat eater, so giving up meat was nothing that caused me any inner strife. I actually found it liberating to search for new meal choices and to discover different ways of eating *sans* meat. My best friend, however, found it a huge struggle to become a vegetarian because of her memorable love for turkey. She tried going veg off and on for a few years before it finally stuck. She would start off eating vegetarian for about a week and then would seesaw between the standard and veg diet. She is now, after three years (and I like to think a little encouragement from Yours Truly), a complete vegetarian who is slowly laying off of dairy. Oh, they grow up so fast!

Lesson: Everyone's journey is a different one! Don't be ashamed of not following a dietary lifestyle 100 percent.

It's always going to be a bit of an exploratory venture to find what works for you. Don't be discouraged if you have cravings for your meaty bygone loves. To this day I still get latent-primitive cravings for a huge slab of steak and mashed potatoes. I can practically feel my Neolithic ancestors throwing rocks at me through the stratums of time. I don't think there's anything wrong with those urges. I feel you should listen to what your body has to say at all times, even if that means re-evaluating your current choices. And if I wanted to deviate from veganism and have a bite of steak, I would.

## ALLOW VEGANISM TO BE A HEALTHY ADDITION TO YOUR DIET

The lifestyle of veganism and vegetarianism should be one you adapt to and adopt voluntarily. You don't have to go all-out vegan if you don't want to all-out commit. Reserve cheese or milk for special occasions, certain days of the week, or holiday treats. Try going vegan for a month to increase your energy. Do it once a year during the summer when eating fresh and light makes you feel great. Be vegan when you *want* to be.

Our cavemen ancestors ate mostly meat, and little else. They didn't drink cow's milk and they certainly didn't eat cheese. They had no processed sugar or grains. Nowadays, there is research to suggest that diets heavy in red or processed meat can lead to heart disease and other health problems. Moderation is the key for most diets, but in a lot of ways, a go at veganism is giving your body the chance to thrive off of what is naturally available from the earth around us.

**VEGANISM AND HEALTH**

This way of eating is not a fad "diet" and should never be treated as one. It is a regimen that must be carefully monitored if adhered to tightly. Just as any other diet, veganism has its challenges. If vegans aren't careful, they will often miss out on vital nutrients such as B12, B6, calcium, iron, folic acid, and protein. Deficiencies can lead to anemia, fatigue, and other health problems.

*Thus, it is always important to talk with your health care provider before switching your eating patterns.*

Enough with that serious stuff, though! If you eat vegan or part-time vegan, and keep a careful eye on what you consume (as with any other diet), you will be healthy, energetic, and feeling spectacular. The whole foods and fresh produce you will consume as a vegan will work toward a better, healthier you.

## What's in a Vegan Pantry, Anyway?

There is a whole WORLD of ingredients one uses specifically in vegan cooking. Arrowroot, egg-replacer, nut milks, and soy yogurt are just to name a few. But there are also old-time favorites that you will use again and again! Here is a helpful list of some things you might find valuable to have in your part-time vegan cabinets:

- *Agave Nectar:* a sweet syrup made from the agave plant of Mexico (the same plant used to make tequila). This is a vegan sweetener that people use in place of traditional sugar. Traditional sugar is often bleached with the use of animal bones. If you wish to be vegan about your traditional sugar (brown or white), just contact the manufacturer and ask if they bleach!

- *Coconut Oil:* Coconut oil can be heated to very high temperatures without changing its molecular form, which makes it perfect for stir-frying. It is also used widely in vegan baking, since it is solid at room temperature, to "set" vegan desserts like "cheese" cakes. To vegan bake with coconut oil, usually you must melt the solid coconut oil into its liquid form. This is simple, and only takes a minute by submerging the coconut oil container in hot water. You can also melt coconut oil for 30 seconds in the microwave.
- *Egg-Replacer:* There are many kinds of "egg-replacer" on the market. Some are specifically sold as mixes in the natural foods section under the name of "egg-replacer mix." Most of the time, eggs are used as a binder in recipes, or they are added to keep the batter moist. Often, the need for moisture can be easily attended to by using bananas, applesauce, jam, or soy yogurt. Remember these items add sugar content to the recipe, and you may wish to adjust recipe sweetness accordingly by adding a little less sweetener (sugar, honey, agave) than the recipe calls for.

**THE** SKINNY **ON . . . Honey**

Honey is the subject of much debate in vegan circles, because during the harvesting of honey, insects are killed. Many vegans consider this a violation of their principles. Others note that bugs are killed in the harvesting of most fruits and vegetables. It's your call as to whether you want to eat it.

If a recipe specifically calls for "egg-replacer," it's best to follow the instructions, as "egg-replacer" works as a binder in baking.
- *Grains:* Grains include barley, millet, bulgur wheat, brown rice, and buckwheat. Use these when you tire of the standard white rice. They have both fiber and protein.
- *Legumes:* Beans, lentils, and sprouted beans are all types of legumes. Also included in this category are black beans, chick peas, kidney beans, black-eyed peas, cannellini beans, and lima beans. Legumes pack a powerful punch of vegan protein.
- *Maple Syrup and Honey:* Here are two other nontraditional natural sweeteners that can take the place of sugar in almost any

recipe. Remember when baking with syrup and honey that since they are liquid your batter may become more runny. Add a little more flour to account for this.

- *Non-Milk Milks:* Soy, rice, almond, hazelnut, coconut, and even hemp milk are all tasty and creamy alternatives to traditional dairy milk. More and more varieties crop up in the supermarket every day. You can even find chocolate, vanilla, chai, and traditional holiday favorites like "eggnog" and autumn spice!

- *Nutritional Yeast:* Despite having the worst food name on the planet, this ingredient is a great source of B12 and protein. It's very inexpensive and lends a sharp "cheesy" flavor to many dishes. Nutritional yeast can also be sprinkled on toast, lettuce, or popcorn.

- *Nuts:* Cashews, pistachios, brazil nuts, macadamias, walnuts, almonds, pecans—you name it! Nuts are great sources of protein and good-for-you fats.

- *Produce:* Meet your new best friend. Go acquaint yourself with the produce section of your grocery store. You will be spending a *lot* of time there. Try to appreciate the fresh flavors of seasonal fruits and veggies, and pick foods for their ripeness and color. Slowly you will get to know the difference between an acorn and a butternut squash, or apricots and peaches! You can use veggies for so many things other than boring old salads—shaved carrots spiced are great substitutes for taco "meat" for example. (Trust me, it's good.)

- *Quinoa:* A South American grain eaten by the ancient Aztecs, quinoa is a powerhouse of proteins and vital nutrients. Quinoa makes a great alternative to rice and can be eaten hot or cold, sweet or savory.

- *Soy Cream:* Coffee lovers everywhere will embrace soy cream. It's also great in many creamy rice or pasta dishes.

- *Spices:* They say variety is the spice of life, but really spices are the spice of life. You can jazz up (or disguise, if that's how you roll) any vegetable on the planet with the flavors of garlic, turmeric, cumin, white and red pepper, basil, parsley, rosemary, cardamom, chicory, chili pepper, coriander, curry powder, ginger, thyme, sage, and tamarind.

- *Tempeh, Seitan, and TVP:* These are terrific substitutes for meat proteins. Tempeh is made from fermented soybeans and has a chewy, crunchy texture that is an excellent addition to salads. Seitan is made from wheat gluten and usually comes in extremely thin slices. It is famous in the vegan world for its meat-like appearance, and like tempeh, it's flavorless and easily absorbs the flavor of any dish. TVP stands for "textured vegetable protein." Really, *who* is coming up with these horrible names? Anyway, TVP is also usually made from soy, and can be found in most of your standard veggie burgers. All can have a distinctly "meaty" texture if prepared properly!

- *Tofu:* Tofu, made from fermented soybeans, is a great protein-filled addition to stir-fries or salads. Tofu can be used in place of eggs in "scrambled eggs" or fritattas. You can also use it to make shakes, smoothies, quiches, pies, love. (Well, maybe not love. Unless you're counting how much you're going to enjoy the food.)

- *Unsweetened/Baking Chocolate, Carob Chips, Cacao Nibs:* Who said vegans can't eat chocolate? Many vegan recipes include baking chocolate (which is purely dark with no milk). Using baking chocolate shavings in a recipe that includes a sweetener like honey or maple syrup gives you the chocolately flavor and preserves the sweetness. Carob chips from the carob plant are nuttier and softer than chocolate, but they are just as good for cookies. Cacao is another plant with a nutty-chocolate taste that adds a great crunch to things like banana bread.

- *Vegan Margarine:* Most regular margarines also happen to be vegan. You can always check the label to be sure. However, many brands are processed on equipment that handle milk, and thus may be "tainted." Simply look for one labeled *vegan* if this concerns you. Many brands of "vegan"-marketed margarine are also available soy-free.

## And How the Hell Do You Find Them?

*Cacao nibs?* Seriously?

Yes, seriously.

It may seem like these things are a little bizarre, but most of the ingredients listed here should be sold at your local grocery store. Natural food chains like Whole Foods carry a few of the more "obscure" items like carob chips and soy yogurt. Check out the resources section for a more complete listing of vegan food suppliers.

In the vegan world, foods that are not catered to vegan buyers yet still remain free of non-vegan ingredients are referred to as "accidentally vegan." Many foods that you would never expect to be vegan just happen to be. Oreos, for one. Many packaged brownie mixes, before you are instructed to add the egg, are also vegan. And now you know how to replace those pesky eggs. Savvy.

On to the cooking!

## Icons Index

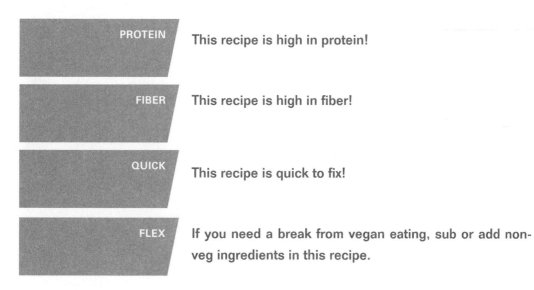

PROTEIN — This recipe is high in protein!

FIBER — This recipe is high in fiber!

QUICK — This recipe is quick to fix!

FLEX — If you need a break from vegan eating, sub or add non-veg ingredients in this recipe.

**CHAPTER 2**

# Dips and Appetizers

## THAT SHALL IMPRESS YOUR FRIENDS

I'm your friend and I'm already impressed. And you haven't even picked up a mixing spoon yet.

# Purely Vegan Chocolate-Hazelnut Spread

**Makes about 2 cups**

Sometimes, the thought of giving up some of your favorite foods is just too much to bear. How can you live without a Hershey's bar or bread and *butter?* For me, the saddest departure I had to make was the long, wistful goodbye to my favorite commercial Chocolate-Hazelnut spread. Think Romeo and Juliet, people. Casablanca. Humphrey and Bacall. Yes, I am still talking about food.

Luckily, there always seems to be a vegan way around these things! This version of Chocolate-Hazelnut Spread is not only delicious, but cuts down on the sugar and is *good* for you! It'll be love at first bite.

2 cups shelled hazelnuts

1 cup almond milk

2 teaspoons vanilla

3 tablespoons canola oil

½ cup dark cocoa powder (Hershey's brand works great)

1 cup powdered sugar

1. Process the nuts until they are a fine meal, or until the mixture begins to stick to the side of the processor and won't mix any longer. This very well may take a few minutes. Be careful not to overheat your processor!

2. Add the almond milk, vanilla, and oil to allow everything to blend further.

3. Add the cocoa and sugar. You can add more sugar depending on your tastes! Keep blending until smooth! Store for up to five days in a tightly sealed container in the fridge.

## PART-TIME TIP

It takes a strong and sturdy food processor with the heart and soul of a tiger to convert any nut into a nut butter. Don't worry if yours is not this adventurous. As a stalwart guardian of the sacred Chocolate-Hazelnut brotherhood, I've designed this recipe to work with any old food processor. If the situation gets sticky, you can always add a dash more canola oil or a few generous pours of almond milk to loosen things up.

# Quick, Homemade, Raw Vegan Pesto

**Yields about 1½ cups**

Traditional pesto is made using pine nuts, but pine nuts seem to be members of a club that is exclusively expensive and posh. I don't know about you, beloved reader, but I usually cannot afford them. Luckily, you can easily substitute walnuts or even almonds for pine nuts. The pesto tastes great, and no one will ever know you swindled them. Which is exactly what we're going for, isn't it?

1 cup walnuts or almonds

½ cup olive oil

½ teaspoon salt

4 cloves garlic, minced

2 to 3 cups packed basil

1 teaspoon ground black pepper

½ cup lemon juice

1 tablespoon nutritional yeast

Process all ingredients in the food processor until it's good and fragrant and tasty. Watch out on the salt, which can overpower the flavor of the basil if you are tempted to add more than ½ teaspoon.

## THE SKINNY ON ... Nutritional Yeast

Apart from most likely having *the* most unappealing food name ever, nutritional yeast is a powerhouse of B vitamins and protein. Many people are initially turned off by its sharp, "cheese"-like flavor, but give it a chance! Not only is it a perfect way for vegans to catch up on their B12 and protein (nearly 8 grams per tablespoon), but it also is used as a substitute for that familiar punch cheese lends to dishes.

To start, try sprinkling a little on top of popcorn or over some lettuce with a little olive oil, salt and pepper. Nutritional yeast can be purchased for as little as $5.00 'round these parts.

# Easy Broccoli Snack Attack

**Serves 1 (multiply ingredients by 4 if serving guests!)**

For when you have the munchies at midnight and your old love, the bag of chips, is texting your phone nonstop. Fiber up. You can basically eat a whole bag of broccoli by yourself and only consume about 100 calories. Good calories! Cut things off with the potato chips! Opportunity is ringing.

1 bag frozen broccoli

1 tablespoon nutritional yeast

1 teaspoon garlic powder

1 tablespoon lemon juice

Dash salt

Pepper to taste

1. Simply defrost broccoli in your chosen manner, and cut it up very finely into tiny pieces. It makes it more fun to eat.

2. Top with all other ingredients and mix well.

# Garlic, Zucchini, Eggplant, and Onion Spread

### Serves 4

Absolutely the best veggies to combine together. The result turns so mouthwatering and luscious. The natural flavors of all of these vegetables are the perfect complements to one another. This dish makes a great party spread for a chopped-up baguette.

6 cloves garlic, minced

4 zucchini, chopped

1 onion, chopped very fine

1 eggplant, chopped

1 tablespoon red wine vinegar

3–4 tablespoons olive oil

Salt and pepper to taste

2 teaspoons nutritional yeast

In a large saucepan, combine all ingredients. Cook over very low heat, stirring continuously for about 15 minutes until completely soft and mixed. Serve hot as a spread!

# Quick Easy Hummus

Makes about 1½ cups

Hummus. Packed with protein. Creamy and delicious. Use it on sandwiches, crackers, or toast! Or, you know, just eat it from the bowl. Plain. As an entire meal. (I've never done it. I swear.)

1 (15-ounce) can chick peas

2 tablespoons tahini paste (see recipe at the end of this chapter)

2 tablespoons olive oil

¾ teaspoon salt

2 teaspoons lemon juice

2 teaspoons minced garlic

Handful of chopped cherry tomatoes for topping

½ tablespoon olive oil for topping

Dash paprika for topping

Simply process all ingredients, except tomatoes, olive oil for topping, and paprika together (using the water from the chick pea can as well). Top with chopped cherry tomatoes, olive oil, and paprika!

## THE SKINNY ON . . . Lactylate

Lots of breads that you may use for toast, dipping, and so forth have an ingredient called *lactylate* (or Sodium Stearoyl Lactylate). It's basically a food-additive used to blend ingredients that don't normally blend (such as oil and water) and it can be synthetic, plant-based, or animal-derived. This is one of those ingredients that can turn a seemingly vegan item non-vegan. If you spot lactylate in any of your pack-aged goods and are concerned, shoot the manufac-turer an e-mail.

# Lean, Mean, Black Bean Guacamole

**Makes 2 cups**

Sometimes, you just can't improve an old favorite. This is not one of those times. Adding black beans into guac is a way to change up your old standby without casting him off as just a bygone lover. Think of it as a fiberful, protein-adding makeover for your favorite Mexican dip.

1 (15-ounce) can black beans, partially drained

3 avocados, pitted

1 tablespoon lemon juice

¼ cup chopped fresh cilantro

½ red onion, diced

1 large tomato, diced

2 cloves garlic, chopped

¼ teaspoon chili powder

¼ teaspoon cumin

¼ teaspoon salt

1. Using a fork (or whatever you have lying around; a fist works), mash the beans up. Don't turn them into mush, but rather leave some texture.

2. Mix all other ingredients into the bowl with the beans.

3. Store in the refrigerator until ready to serve! You can save the scrumptious covered leftovers for up to three days in the fridge.

# Baked Zucchini Fries

Serves 2

Try not to thank yourself after you bake this incredible French-fry substitute. I mean, should we even *call* it a substitute? How about new, fantastic, love-of-your-life? These fries mimic your traditional fast-food favorites, but they are also healthy, crunchy, and packed with the nutritional benefits of olive oil. You know, heart-stopping—in a good way.

2 zucchini (or 1 per person)

½ cup whole wheat flour

½ teaspoon garlic

½ teaspoon paprika

½ teaspoon onion powder

Salt to taste

Cracked pepper to taste

1 tablespoon nutritional yeast

¼ cup olive oil

1. Preheat oven to 450°F.

2. Wash and cut zucchini into 2" strips. I prefer to leave the skin on because that's where all the nutrients live.

3. Mix whole wheat flour, garlic, paprika, onion powder, salt, pepper, and nutritional yeast in a small bowl. Set aside.

4. Lay the zucchini fries out on a cookie sheet, brushing with a very light coating of olive oil.

5. Toss fries into the bowl with the flour/seasoning mix. After they are coated, place on cookie sheet again.

6. Lightly brush the coated fries with olive oil once more, and bake for 15 minutes. Serve with marinara or vegan "alfredo" sauce!

# Mango Citrus Salsa

**Makes 2 cups**

Wish you were hanging out on the beach? So do I. But here I am, writing down this recipe for you, so you can *pretend* you're at the beach. You: squinting from the bright and brilliant sun, standing in front of crystalline waters and watching the turquoise waves drop and pull away. The heady, floral caress of wind in the palm trees and your hair. A cold drink in your hand. And in the other: delicate fingers grasping a chip, plunging it into this cool, refreshing salsa. (Really sold this one, didn't I? I tried!)

1 mango, chopped

2 tangerines (or clementines), chopped

½ sweet red bell pepper

½ red onion, minced

3 cloves garlic, minced

½ jalapeno pepper, minced

2 tablespoons lime juice

½ teaspoon salt

½ teaspoon cayenne pepper

½ teaspoon black pepper

3 tablespoons chopped cilantro

1. Mix all ingredients together. Well, that just about does it, folks.

2. Let sit for about fifteen minutes to allow the flavors to meet and greet. And then interrupt the party without haste.

# Roasted Chick Peas, Please

Serves 2

Crunchy. Tasty. Feels like you're eating a snack that should be bad for you but somehow it is suspiciously good for you. All in a day's work, my friend.

2 (15-ounce) cans garbanzo beans, drained

2 teaspoons cumin

1 teaspoon salt

1 teaspoon ground black pepper

1 teaspoon garlic

1 teaspoon paprika

1 teaspoon turmeric powder

1. Preheat oven to 450°F.

2. Simply season chick peas with spices and place them evenly onto a cookie sheet.

3. Cook for approximately 45 minutes, mixing once. Let cool for 5 minutes before eating.

# (You're) Hot Artichoke Spinach Dip

## Serves 8

Traditional spinach dips are loaded with calories and unforgiving fats. Luckily for all of us, this version combines all of the creaminess and flavor of the original with "cheesy" goodness, vegan-style. Spread it onto some store-bought mini-toasts or some toasted pita bread. You'll impress your guests, and your damn fine hips will thank you.

1 (12-ounce) package frozen spinach, thawed

1 (14-ounce) can artichoke hearts, drained

¼ cup vegan margarine (try Earth Balance)

¼ cup whole wheat flour

2 cups almond milk

½ cup nutritional yeast

1 teaspoon garlic powder

1½ teaspoons onion powder

½ teaspoon white pepper

¼ teaspoon salt

1. Preheat oven to 350°F.

2. Purée spinach and artichokes together and set aside.

3. In a saucepan, melt the vegan margarine and spoon in the flour a tablespoon at a time. Keep stirring slowly until the mixture thickens. (Don't get impatient like I do.)

4. Remove the saucepan from the heat. In a large bowl, combine the margarine mix, the artichoke-and-spinach puree, and the remainder of the ingredients.

5. Place mixture in an oven-safe dish (or you'll be enjoying Artichoke, Plastic, and Spinach Dip) and bake for 20 minutes. Serve hot!

## THE SKINNY ON . . . Vegan Margarine

Most margarines are in fact vegan in the sense that they use no animal-derived products. However, they may be manufactured in places where milk products are dealt with, so potentially they could have been "contaminated" with whey or lactose. If you are looking for 100 percent certified vegan margarine, just check the labels. Otherwise, use the "accidentally vegan" brand you have in the fridge.

# Easy Apple Butter

**Makes about 1 cup**

A sweet, thick spread that can be used on toast or fruit. Try using it as a dip for bananas or spreading it on a bagel.

2 tablespoons vegan margarine

1½ pounds red apples, peeled and cored

2½ cups mulled cider

1 teaspoon nutmeg

1 teaspoon honey

1 tablespoon orange juice

1. Preheat oven to 250°F.

2. Melt margarine in a large pot. Add peeled apples. Stir and cover for 5 minutes.

3. Add mulled cider. Bring to a boil and then allow to simmer for 30 minutes. Mash mushy apples with a spoon until they come apart, then cook for another 2 minutes. Remove from heat.

4. Blend the mixture in a food processor until smooth. Add nutmeg, honey, and orange juice. Process again.

5. Smooth the mixture onto a cookie sheet and bake for two hours, stirring occasionally. Allow to thicken. Store in an airtight container in the fridge for up to a week!

# Parsley and Onion Dip

**Serves 6**

Be prepare to get addicted. This tangy, lively dip is going to be the hit of your party. Dip pretzels into it, veggies, crisps, chips—hell, a spoon works, too. People will have no idea you're missing the fat-laden sour cream that is usually the main ingredient of onion dips. But you won't be missing it at all. Clever minx.

1 onion, chopped (yellow works best)

3 cloves garlic, minced

1 tablespoon olive oil

1 block firm tofu, well pressed

½ teaspoon onion powder

3 teaspoons lemon juice

1 teaspoon apple cider vinegar

¼ cup fresh parsley, chopped

2 tablespoons fresh chives

¼ teaspoon salt

1. In a large saucepan, sauté onion and garlic in the olive oil for about 4 minutes. Make sure the onions are soft and slightly translucent. Remove pan from burner and let mixture cool.

2. Process the onion/garlic mixture along with the tofu, onion powder, and lemon juice.

3. Spoon into a bowl and mix all other ingredients in manually. I know you can do it. Consider it your exercise for the day. Serve immediately and store for up to two days.

## THE SKINNY ON ... Pressing Tofu

Pressing tofu is the process by which you drain the tofu of extra water. This allows it to be drier, denser, and more able to absorb flavor. Flavor is a good thing, eh? Simply lay your block of tofu out on a couple of paper towels, hand pressing another paper towel to the top of the tofu block in order to remove visible water. Next, replace all paper towels and set a heavy object (such as a can) on top of the tofu for a good twenty minutes. The end result? A dry block that's ready for a flavor-infusion! I bet you never thought tofu could be this exciting.

# Homemade Tahini

**Makes 1 cup**

We've made quick-and-easy hummus, but one of the ingredients, tahini paste, is a bit on the expensive side. Here's a recipe for homemade tahini to use in your homemade hummus—very pioneering of you. Very 1849. You can also use the tahini as an ingredient in a salad dressing, or even as a dip by itself. Ah, innovation.

2 cups sesame seeds

½ cup olive oil

½ teaspoon paprika (optional)

¼ teaspoon salt (optional)

½ teaspoon cracked black pepper (optional)

1. Heat oven to 350°F. On a baking sheet, lay the sesame seeds out and bake them for about 6 minutes. Make sure to stir them once.

2. After the seeds cool down, throw them into the food processor with the olive oil, making sure to get the consistency as creamy as possible. If your food processor is throwing a conniption, add a tiny bit more olive oil.

3. Add the salt, paprika, and cracked black pepper if you are using this as a stand-alone dip. Otherwise just leave it be.

# CHAPTER 3

# Easy Breakfasts

## FOR PEOPLE WHO ARE ON THE GO AND MORE TIME-CONSUMING BREAKFASTS FOR THOSE OF US WHO ARE LAZY AND HAVE LOTS OF TIME FOR EATING

I just may be included in the latter group, but I'm not going to give the game away.

# Crepes, for When You're Feeling Lazy

Serves 4

Crepes have to be the absolute simplest thing to make. It's a little hard to go flipping them about, but once you've got the hang of it, I promise that this will be your go-to recipe of the month. You can fill them with sweet fruits or savory onions, tomatoes, and garlic. Either way, they're a great light meal you can assemble with anything you have on hand.

1 cup whole wheat or white whole wheat flour

¾ cup almond milk

½ cup water

2 teaspoons sugar

1 teaspoon vanilla

¼ cup vegan margarine, melted

¼ teaspoon salt

Whatever fillings you have in mind, Master Chef. Enough of each ingredient to fill a small cereal bowl should give you enough options

1. Whisk all ingredients except fillings together and refrigerate for about an hour. Remove and mix again.

2. Allow skillet to heat on medium for approximately one minute before starting to cook. Lightly grease skillet with vegan margarine. Swirl approximately ¼ cup of batter into the pan so that all edges are covered. Cook on medium-high heat for a minute. Use a spatula to flip. Cook the other side. Crepes will be finished when very lightly browned. Repeat with remaining batter.

3. Fill 'em up and fold 'em! Use your creative genius. Serve immediately.

PROTEIN
FIBER
# Black Quinoa Breakfast Cereal

Serves 4

Do you gag at the thought of boring oatmeal? Crash after a sugar-laden breakfast cereal and are near comatose by the time 11:00 A.M. rolls around?

This black quinoa breakfast cereal is a perfect way to start your day. Packed full of protein, antioxidants, and essential vitamins, it'll keep you running straight past the afternoon slump. If you don't have quinoa chilling around your house, use brown rice. It's just as good!

1 cup black quinoa (or regular quinoa)

1½ cups water

1½ cups sliced strawberries

2 sliced bananas

½ cup wolfberries (goji berries) or blueberries

¾ cup unsalted raw cashews

2 tablespoons maple syrup

About ½ cup almond or soy milk

1. In a large saucepan, combine quinoa with water. Bring to boil and then reduce to a simmer. Let simmer until all the water is evaporated, approximately 20 minutes. The quinoa should be completely cooked. It's okay if it's a little crunchy!

2. Drain quinoa. Add fruit, cashews, and maple syrup. Top with your favorite almond or soy milk!

PROTEIN
FIBER
QUICK
FLEX
# Easy Vegan Breakfast Parfait

Serves 2

Vegans can *so* eat yogurt. But you'll be searching for those made from soy, not cow or goat's milk. There are so many variations of soy yogurt these days—so many flavors—you won't be hard-pressed to find a new favorite.

¼ cup flax meal

2 (6-ounce) containers soy yogurt (any flavor)

2 tablespoons maple syrup

½ cup granola

½ cup sliced bananas or strawberries

1. Mix flax, soy yogurt, and maple syrup together.

2. For 2 servings, use 2 different containers. For 1 big serving, use 1 bigger container. Layer in this order: yogurt mixture, granola, fruit, until everything is used up.

# Carob-Peanut Butter Smoothie

Serves 2

Dear Reader:

For those who constantly crave the creamy, nutty goodness of peanut butter and the subtle, hearty flavor of carob, and for those who wish to have an energizing, protein-filled smoothie to replace those bottled post-workout protein drinks, we cut down on the sugar and gave you some potassium. And you didn't even have to ask.

Love, Peanut Butter

8 ice cubes

2 bananas

2 tablespoons all-natural peanut butter

2 tablespoons carob powder (or crushed carob chips or cocoa powder)

1 cup almond milk

Splash of apple juice

Blend all ingredients in a blender or food processor and you're golden. Serve immediately.

# Homemade Almond Milk

**Makes 4 cups**

The almond milk, soy milk, or rice milk that you purchase at the supermarket is usually loaded with sugar. I find that fruit and cereal contain enough sugar already, so why should I be adding more to my smoothies or breakfasts? Plus homemade is the freshest you can get—sort of like milking your own cow. But without the cow. Or the milk. Or the hay. Or the fertilizer on your shoes.

1 cup raw, unsalted almonds (or any other nut), soaked overnight

4 cups fresh water for blending

½ teaspoon vanilla (or any other extract)

1 tablespoon sweetener of your choice (maple syrup, honey, agave, sugar)

A pinch salt

1. Process the soaked nuts and the 4 cups water until there are no lumps left.

2. Strain the puree through a cheese-cloth in order to catch any remaining pieces.

3. Stir in extract and sweetener, along with salt. Store in the fridge for up to a week.

# Top of the Morning Cashew Butter Wrap

**Makes 1 wrap**

Soft, filling, and sweet but not overly saccharine—these breakfast wraps will have everyone around you as green as the hills of Ireland. Perfect if you stumbled out of bed after hitting snooze too many times and have to make a mad dash for your car. After all, you don't want to be late on an empty stomach, do you?

2 tablespoons cashew butter (or any other nut butter)

1 whole wheat flour tortilla

2 tablespoons Kashi Honey Sunshine Cereal (or any other)

A handful of blackberries

1½ bananas, sliced thin

¼ teaspoon allspice

1 tablespoon raisins

½ tablespoon maple syrup or agave nectar

1. Spread nut butter onto the tortilla. Layer with cereal, blackberries, and banana slices.

2. Add the allspice and raisins and drizzle with maple syrup or agave. Fold or roll up the wrap tightly.

3. Warm in the microwave for about 12 seconds with the seam of the wrap facing down. Mix and match ingredients at your will! Use whatever you have lying around the house.

## PART-TIME TIP
Fiber helps prevent the absorption of fat.

# Peach-Thyme Muffins

**Makes 18 muffins**

Talk about your potentially random combinations, right? I promise the sharp tartness of peach and smooth, leafy taste of thyme really do make the perfect complement. They're like Lewis and Clark, or George Washington and the Continental Army. Maybe a little less militant than the latter, but certainly as adventurous as the former. Start your day off like a trail-blazing, intrepid explorer of unmarked lands! These muffins are delightfully aromatic and pair perfectly with a glass of OJ and a drizzle of honey.

2 cups whole wheat flour

1 cup white whole wheat flour

¾ to 1 cup sugar

½ teaspoon salt

1 tablespoon baking soda

½ cup peach jam

1½ cups almond milk

1 teaspoon lemon extract

¼ cup fresh thyme

1 cup peaches, diced

Honey for drizzling

1. Preheat oven to 400°F.

2. Combine both flours, sugar, salt, and baking soda in a large bowl. Set aside.

3. In a different bowl, whisk together the jam, almond milk, and lemon extract. Make sure to mix well!

4. Slowly add the wet mix to the dry mix. Stir as you go.

5. Fold thyme into mixture.

6. Fold peaches in gently.

7. Grease muffin tins with vegan margarine and add batter so each cup is about two-thirds full.

8. Bake for 25 minutes and then cool. Very gently remove from tin and drizzle with honey.

## PART-TIME TIP

White whole wheat flour is a good way to trick (yes, we're devious) your friends and family into thinking that they're not eating whole wheat. Cross my heart, they won't even notice. It's ground much finer than regular whole wheat flour, which means it's smoother to the taste and touch. King Arthur flour brand makes a spectacular White Whole Wheat baking flour.

# Whole Wheat Brilliant Blueberry Muffins

**Makes 18 muffins**

Brainfood. There's a lot to be said for getting your mind running in the morning without the help of caffeine. The antioxidants in blueberries are going to keep you looking stellar and feeling fabulous. Eating one of these nutritious, filling muffins will give you some fiber and keep you away from those sugar-laden, fat-filled breakfast combos. Now, that's a smart cookie.

2 cups whole wheat flour

1 cup white whole wheat or all-purpose flour

¾ cup oats

1¼ cups brown sugar

1 tablespoon baking soda

1 teaspoon salt

1½ cups almond milk

½ cup applesauce

½ teaspoon vanilla

2 cups blueberries

Powdered sugar for garnish

1. Preheat oven to 400°F.

2. Combine flours, oats, brown sugar, baking soda, and salt in a large bowl.

3. In a different bowl, combine the almond milk, applesauce, and vanilla. Whisk with a fork.

4. Add the wet mixture to the dry mixture. Gently fold in blueberries.

5. Grease muffin tins with vegan margarine and add batter so each cup is about two-thirds full.

6. Cook for 20 minutes. Cool for 10 minutes and remove gently from pan. Top with a little powdered sugar.

## THE SKINNY ON . . . Almond Milk

There are various kinds of non-dairy milk available. Soy, rice, hemp, almond—and who knows what variations people are coming up with these days! Rice milk is the thinnest, and soy milk is the most common. However, there are some excellent versions of almond milk on the store shelves these days, my favorite brand being Almond Breeze. I try to watch my soy intake and to limit it when I cook, which is why most of these recipes use almond milk. However, feel free to substitute according to your preferences!

# Down-Home Vegan Biscuits

**Makes 12 biscuits**

There is nothing like a buttered biscuit to warm my heart and have me seeing fireflies in the summer heat of the south. Smear jam on them, soak them with vegan margarine, or saturate them in honey. I sort of let loose when it comes to biscuits. And eat the whole batch. Every time. What can I say? Nobody's perfect.

⅔ cup almond milk

1 teaspoon apple cider vinegar

2 cups whole wheat or white flour

1 tablespoon baking powder

½ teaspoon salt

5 tablespoons cold vegan margarine

1. Preheat oven to 425°F.

2. Pour the almond milk and apple cider vinegar into a small bowl. Set aside for 5 minutes to allow to curdle.

3. In a large bowl, mix the flour, baking powder, and salt.

4. Cut in the cold margarine with a fork. Work at the dough until it is divided into small pea-sized segments and the margarine is no longer visible.

5. Add the wet mixture to the dry mixture and knead by hand.

6. Sprinkle flour on a hard surface and roll out dough until it is about ½" thick. Use a drinking glass to cut dough into ¾" rounds. Place on ungreased cookie sheet. If you like, brush a little melted margarine over the top of each biscuit before it cooks.

7. Cook for about 13 minutes until the bottoms of the biscuits are lightly browned.

# Easy Breakfast Blackberry Bread Pudding

Serves 1

The easiest and most delicious breakfast you'll ever make. Way more exciting than boring-beige-blasé oatmeal, and just as tasty. The perfect comfort breakfast food for a chilly spring morning or an autumn afternoon. Feel free to substitute any fruit you have lying around instead of the blackberries. Peach, banana, raspberries, or blueberries would all work great.

2 slices whole wheat bread

½ cup almond milk

½ teaspoon vanilla

½ pint blackberries

1 tablespoon honey

1 teaspoon jam (any flavor)

Brown sugar for sprinkling

1. Toast the bread and tear into small pieces, tossing in a stovetop pan.

2. Add almond milk and vanilla to pan and heat on medium so the milk is warmed, but not simmering. Mix often.

3. Add in blackberries, honey, and jam and continue to heat for 10 minutes until bread is saturated with milk and excess is mostly evaporated.

4. Sprinkle with brown sugar and serve hot.

# You Say Banaana, I Say Baanana Bread

**Makes 1 loaf**

When you cook banana bread, make sure to use bananas that are almost ready to see the rubbish bin. The mushier and less edible they seem—the better banana bread they'll make. This bread is moist and chewy, with a crunch that'll make you, um, . . . go bananas.

4 ripe bananas

⅓ cup almond milk

1 teaspoon vanilla

⅔ cup maple syrup

4 tablespoons cacao nibs

½ teaspoon apple cider vinegar

2 cups whole wheat flour

1 teaspoon baking powder

½ teaspoon baking soda

½ teaspoon salt

¼ teaspoon cinnamon

¼ teaspoon nutmeg

Walnuts to sprinkle on top

1. Preheat oven to 350°F. Grease a loaf pan with vegan margarine.

2. In a large bowl, mash together the bananas, almond milk, vanilla, maple syrup, cacao nibs, and apple cider vinegar. Mix very well.

3. Using another bowl, mix together the flour, baking powder, baking soda, salt, cinnamon, and nutmeg. Combine with the banana mixture, blending evenly.

4. Pour batter into loaf pan and sprinkle walnuts on top. Cook for 55 minutes or until a toothpick inserted into the loaf comes out clean. Let cool and devour.

# Cashew Cream with Baby Tomatoes on Multigrain Toast

Serves 2

When you're in the mood for a savory breakfast, please do stop here. Sweet can sometimes quickly turn to sickly sweet, and brunch is always best served sans sugar, if you ask me.

Try out this elegant little number and convince yourself that you're royalty. It just seems to me like something served in Windsor Palace. Little toasts and tomatoes and tea and . . . well. Let's not get carried away. It *is* only brunch time, after all. Lord knows we have to save our fantasies for dessert.

1 pint baby tomatoes

2 tablespoons balsamic vinegar

½ teaspoon salt

Dash cracked pepper

2 slices thick whole wheat bread

1½ cups unsalted raw cashews, soaked for 1 hour or more and drained

½ cup water

1½ tablespoons lemon juice

3–4 teaspoons apple cider vinegar

¼ cup fresh chopped basil

2 tablespoons olive oil

1. Chop baby tomatoes in half. In a small bowl, whisk together balsamic vinegar, salt, and cracked black pepper. Allow tomatoes to marinate for 15 minutes.

2. Toast the two slices of thick whole wheat bread in the toaster, or for a few minutes in a warm oven.

3. Process the cashews, water, lemon juice, and apple cider vinegar until the consistency is creamy. The taste should be sharp and pleasant.

4. Layer each toast slice with chopped basil and marinated tomatoes. Drizzle with olive oil and top with a dollop of the previously processed cashew cream.

# Strawberry Protein Smoothie

Serves 2 (that's two for you, ahem)

Great for those hot summer evenings when you're craving something sweet and cold. But this one won't make you curse yourself in the morning. And hey, you'll get some protein out of it! Things are always better if you can tell yourself you got protein out of it.

½ cup strawberries

½ block silken tofu

1 banana

¾ cup apple juice

3–4 ice cubes

1 tablespoon agave or honey

Blend, baby, blend.

## THE SKINNY ON . . . Agave Nectar

A little-known fact about agave nectar is that while the glycemic index is very low, and thus will not spike blood sugar, agave has been recorded to have varying levels of fructose—from 56–92 percent! The remaining percentage is made up of glucose. This is higher than even the fructose content of some high fructose corn syrups! I say, everything is fine in moderation. But if you are concerned about fructose levels, consider swapping out agave nectar for maple syrup on occasion.

# Morning Cereal Bars

**Makes 12 bars**

They don't necessarily have to be eaten in the morning. I find they're quite fabulous all day long. Crunchy, sweet, and easy to be eaten on-the-run, you can store them in the fridge until they're completely gone. And what's best, you can pronounce all the ingredients.

3 cups your favorite breakfast cereal (I recommend Kashi brands)

1 cup peanut butter, all-natural (Smuckers works great)

⅓ cup tahini

1 cup maple syrup

½ teaspoon vanilla

2 cups muesli

½ cup flax meal or wheat germ

½ cup raisins

1. Grease an 8"x13" baking pan.

2. Take the cereal of your choice and crush it into small pieces. It's far less messy to do this in a bowl or in a plastic bag. Leave to the side.

3. In a pot set on low, mix the peanut butter, tahini, and maple syrup together for about 4 minutes.

4. Remove pan from heat. Mix in all other ingredients, including the crushed cereal.

5. Press mixture into your greased pan and stick in the fridge for a good 45 minutes before cutting in squares!

## PART-TIME TIP

It is crucial to store ground flax or flax seed in the refrigerator or it will go rancid.

# Chili Masala Tofu Scramble

Serves 4

Scrambling tofu is a great way to recreate the taste and texture of scrambled eggs. It's great as leftovers, too! Eat them in a sandwich for a brunch. Make some vegan pancakes, pour a fresh glass of almond milk . . . and you'll be ready for anything.

1 pound block firm tofu, pressed (see Chapter 2 for simple instructions)

1 small onion, diced

2 cloves garlic, minced

2 tablespoons olive oil

1 small red chili pepper, minced

1 green bell pepper, chopped

¾ cup sliced mushrooms

1 tablespoon of soy sauce

1 teaspoon curry powder

½ teaspoon cumin

¼ teaspoon turmeric

1 teaspoon nutritional yeast

1. Cut or mash pressed tofu into 1"-thick cubes.

2. Sauté onion and garlic in olive oil for two minutes on medium heat.

3. Add the tofu and chili pepper, bell pepper, and mushrooms. Stir to mix everything well.

4. Add all other ingredients except the nutritional yeast. Cook tofu and stir mixture until tofu is browned, about 8 minutes.

5. Remove from heat, sprinkle with nutritional yeast and serve.

## PART-TIME TIP

There are lots of variations you can do with a tofu scramble! Think of your favorite combos. Try spinach and broccoli, vegan cheese and tomato, or a spicy southwestern tofu take on huevos rancheros.

# CHAPTER 4

# Salad Dressings

## THAT ARE EASIER THAN PIE

Pie may be offended by this chapter title. But I trust Pie will get over it.

# Raspberry Vinaigrette

Makes 1¼ cups

Sweet, sharp, and perfect for a salad that is full of crisp, summery greens. Toss in some cranberries or some strawberries, add some pecans or almonds, or even serve with shredded coconut and watermelon.

¼ cup balsamic or raspberry vinegar

2 tablespoons lime juice

¼ cup raspberry preserves

2 tablespoons Dijon mustard

½ teaspoon sugar

¼ teaspoon nutmeg

¼ cup olive oil

Salt and pepper to taste

1. Process all ingredients except the olive oil, salt, and pepper.

2. Slowly add oil, drop by drop, processing on high speed.

3. Season with salt and pepper.

# Creamy Miso Sesame Dressing

Makes 1 cup

Use this dressing on noodles or on arugula. Get fancy by adding some pine nuts or tangerines. The brilliant tang will wake up your mouth, and maybe even some conversation about how remarkable and talented you are.

¼ cup miso

2 tablespoons rice wine vinegar

¼ cup soy sauce

2 tablespoons sesame oil

½ cup soy milk

2 tablespoons lime juice

½ teaspoon white pepper

Simply process all ingredients. Easy-peasy!

# Vegan Mayonnaise

**Makes 1 cup**

There are many kinds of commercial vegan mayonnaise available nowadays, but of course, I feel the DIY kind is best. This way, you know exactly what you're putting into your food and it'll taste the freshest that it possibly can. Plus, vegan mayonnaise is low in fat and just as tasty as regular mayo. You can also use this as another excuse to pat yourself on the back! You know I love those! Congratulate yourself while simultaneously spreading it on sandwiches, or use it as the base of other recipes to come.

1 (12-ounce) block silken tofu

1½ tablespoons lemon juice

1 teaspoon mustard

1½ teaspoons apple cider vinegar

1 teaspoon sugar

¾ teaspoon onion powder

½ teaspoon salt

⅓ cup canola oil

1. Process all ingredients excluding the oil.

2. Add the oil *very* slowly. This is crucial. Quite literally one drop at a time, and process on high speed.

3. Allow to sit in the fridge for an hour before serving, and voila! Well done, Master Chef.

# Asian Dipping Sauce

**Makes ¼ cup**

If you haven't brushed up on your Asian cooking chops in the infinite spare time you have doing other things like studying physics or building an artificial heart, don't worry. This is a recipe my dog could figure out. And my dog is pretty stupid. (Sorry, Taz. Be honest, you know it's the truth.) Dip veggie sushi or edamame into it. Or serve it alongside tofu and steamed vegetables like broccoli and onions.

¼ cup soy sauce

2 tablespoons rice vinegar

2 teaspoons sesame oil

1 teaspoon sugar

1 teaspoon fresh ginger, minced

2 cloves garlic, minced and crushed

¼ teaspoon crushed red pepper

Simply whisk everything together. Done and done. Serve immediately.

# Dairy-Free Ranch Dressing

Makes 1 cup

A recipe that shall have cows smiling everywhere. This is one of those things that makes you say *ah!* when you taste it. It's really remarkable when you start to discover that everything *really does* have a vegan alternative. So get your celery and carrots ready. Today they shall meet their doom.

1 cup Vegan Mayonnaise (see previous for recipe)

¼ cup soy milk

1 tablespoon Dijon mustard

1 tablespoon lemon juice

1 teaspoon onion powder

¾ teaspoon garlic powder

2 tablespoons minced chives

Mix everything together with a whisk, adding the chives last. Store in the refrigerator in a closed container for up to a week.

# Asian Ranch Dressing

Makes ⅔ cup

An exotic twist on a classic favorite. Very global of you. Very trendy.

½ cup Vegan Mayonnaise (see previous for recipe)

⅓ cup rice vinegar

¼ cup soy sauce

2 tablespoons sesame oil

2 teaspoons sugar

½ teaspoon powdered ginger

¾ teaspoon garlic powder

1 tablespoon chopped fresh chives

Mix all ingredients together. Put chives in last.

# To Thai for Orange Peanut Dressing

Makes ¾ cup

Mmmmmm. This is my favorite dressing of all time. I love the savory-sweetness and the rich full flavor. Tangy and spicy, this Indonesian peanut sauce makes a yummy dip for veggies or a marinade for tofu.

¼ cup peanut butter, room temperature

¼ cup orange juice

2 tablespoons soy sauce

2 tablespoons rice vinegar

1 tablespoon water

½ teaspoon garlic powder

½ teaspoon sugar

¼ teaspoon crushed red pepper

Simply whisk everything together and you're ready to party. Serve immediately.

# Old Reliable: Balsamic Vinaigrette

**Makes 1 cup**

The old standby of salad dressings. Always there for you when the ranch or the blue cheese has gone bad. Always there for you at a neighbor's house when you dislike all of the other selections. An ode to balsamic vinaigrette. Let's hear it for him.

½ cup balsamic vinegar

¼ cup olive oil

1 tablespoon Dijon mustard

¼ teaspoon salt

¼ teaspoon black pepper

½ teaspoon dried basil

½ teaspoon dried parsley

Mix all ingredients together, really blending well. Like, beat the hell out of it. As they say, oil and vinegar are reluctant frenemies. Store in the fridge in a closed container for up to three days.

# CHAPTER 5

# Salads

## THAT WON'T LEAF YOU WISHING FOR MORE

Your coworkers will be green with envy. Of course, it's up to you whether you share or not.

# Cucumber Cilantro Salad

Serves 2

A very refreshing, simple salad to make. Mixing the freshness of cucumbers with the creaminess of yogurt is both satisfying and light. Use this unusual salad to cool you off on a hot day, and pair it with a glass of white wine.

4 cucumbers, diced

2 tomatoes, chopped

½ red onion, diced small

1 cup soy yogurt, plain

1 tablespoon lemon juice

2 tablespoons chopped fresh cilantro

½ teaspoon cayenne pepper

Salt and pepper to taste

Simply toss all ingredients together, stir, and chill in the fridge for about 2 hours. Toss once more before serving.

# Lean, Mean, Kidney Bean and Chick Pea Salad

Serves 6

Fiberful and packed with protein, these two delicious beans are the perfect complement to a light, tangy, vinegar-based marinade. A great side dish for vegan ribs (yep, those exist; look for them in the vegan frozen section), or cornbread.

¼ cup olive oil

¼ cup red wine vinegar

½ teaspoon paprika

2 tablespoons lemon juice

1 (14-ounce) can chick peas, drained

1 (14-ounce) can dark red kidney beans, drained

½ cup sliced black olives

1 (8-ounce) can corn, drained

½ red onion, chopped

1 tablespoon fresh chopped parsley

Salt and pepper to taste

1. Whisk the olive oil, vinegar, paprika, and lemon juice.

2. Combine remaining ingredients in another bowl, mixing thoroughly. Pour olive oil mixture over. Mix again.

3. Let set for 30 minutes, in fridge or otherwise. Serve.

# Edamame Salad

Serves 4

Edamame will save your life. Keep a bag of it around for meals, snacks, late night binges, breakfast, lunch, brunch, sleepwalking. It is the most delicious and healthy treat, easy to cook, easy to eat, easy to clean up. Basically, they are too incredible to describe properly. Like you, dear reader. My, my, don't you have a lot in common.

2 cups edamame, thawed and drained (shelled or unshelled, your choice)

1 red bell pepper, diced

2 tablespoons chopped fresh cilantro

2 tablespoons olive oil

2 tablespoons red wine vinegar

1 teaspoon soy sauce

1 teaspoon chili powder

2 teaspoons lemon juice

Salt and pepper to taste

1. In one bowl, mix edamame, bell pepper, and cilantro.

2. In a different bowl, whisk together all other ingredients. Pour mixture over edamame. This will taste absolutely scrumptious.

3. Allow to sit in fridge for about an hour before serving. The beans will absorb the flavor and be delicious. If you choose not to use shelled edamame, the shell of the bean will absorb the flavor of the sauce, and you'll taste it as you bite them out.

# Vegan Potato Pesto Salad

Serves 4

Were you addicted to egg/potato salad before you decided to give veganism a date night? You know what? So was I. I was absolutely *addicted*, and I believed that in my heart, nothing could ever replace it. Luckily, I was wrong. This potato salad, served cold, is creamy and zesty and perfect for a picnic either outside or on the living room floor, your choice.

¼ cup Italian dressing or Old Reliable: Balsamic Vinaigrette (see Chapter 4 for recipe)

¼ cup Vegan Mayonnaise (see Chapter 4 for recipe)

½ cup vegan pesto (see Chapter 2 for recipe)

1 red bell pepper, chopped

½ red onion, chopped

2 pounds red or blue potatoes, cooked and diced

¼ cup parsley, chopped

⅓ cup black olives

Salt and pepper to taste

1. Mix together dressing and mayonnaise.

2. Combine all remaining ingredients. You totally own this. Go you.

# Soy and Sesame Coleslaw Salad

Serves 4

Forget the mayo. This coleslaw gets its flavor from soy sauce and maple syrup. Throw a little tofu in to make a complete meal.

1 head Napa cabbage, shredded

1 carrot, grated

2 green onions, chopped

1 red bell pepper, sliced thin

2 tablespoons olive oil

2 tablespoons apple cider vinegar

2 teaspoons soy sauce

½ teaspoon sesame oil

2 tablespoons maple syrup

2 tablespoons sesame seeds

1. Mix cabbage, carrot, onions, and bell pepper in a bowl. Set aside.

2. In a small bowl, whisk together remaining ingredients except sesame seeds. Drizzle over cabbage mixture. Top with sesame seeds.

# Eggless "Egg" Salad

Serves 4

This recipe is just COOL. I mean, it's eggless—yet it tastes *exactly* like egg salad.

1 pound block firm tofu

1 pound block silken tofu

½ cup vegan mayo

⅓ cup sweet pickle relish

¾ teaspoon apple cider vinegar

2 tablespoons minced onion

1½ tablespoons Dijon mustard

2 tablespoons chopped chives

1 tablespoon fresh chopped dill

1 teaspoon paprika

1.  In a bowl, mash up all ingredients with a fork except for the paprika.

2.  Chill for 15 minutes, garnish with paprika, and serve on bulky white rolls with lettuce and tomato. Or just eat as is! Mmmm.

# Deli-Style Macaroni Salad

Serves 6

This pasta salad is made using Vegan Mayonnaise (see Chapter 4 for recipe). Make sure to salt the water generously when you cook the pasta! This is the secret to making it delicious and rich.

2 cups cooked whole wheat macaroni

1 carrot, diced small

½ cup green peas

½ cup corn

1 rib celery, diced

½ cup Vegan Mayonnaise

1½ tablespoons mustard

2 tablespoons apple cider vinegar

2 tablespoons pickle relish

2 teaspoons sugar

1 tablespoon chopped fresh dill

Salt and pepper to taste

1. In a large bowl, mix macaroni, carrot, peas, corn, and celery. It will be so colorful. This makes me happy.

2. In another bowl, mix together the mayonnaise, mustard, apple cider vinegar, pickle relish, and sugar. Stir in the dill and salt and pepper. Add to the macaroni mixture and stir together.

3. Chill for 2 hours, and serve!

# Hot German Dijon Potato Salad

Serves 4

You ever have those days when you say, "Man, I really feel like a hot German Dijon potato salad?" Yeah, me neither. But I promise you will in the future if you try this.

4 large potatoes, cooked and cooled

½ yellow onion, sliced thin

2 tablespoons olive oil

⅓ cup water

⅓ cup white vinegar

1 tablespoon Dijon mustard

1 tablespoon whole wheat flour

1 teaspoon sugar

2 scallions, chopped

Salt and pepper to taste

1. Cut potatoes into cubes and set aside.

2. In medium saucepan set on medium-high heat, sauté onions in olive oil for about 3 minutes.

3. Add water, vinegar, mustard, flour, and sugar. Stir. Simmer, and let thicken for 1 minute.

4. Lower the heat and then add the cubed potatoes and the scallions. Stir for a few minutes until it's heated through. Season a bit with salt and pepper, and serve!

# Lemon Cumin Potato Salad

**Serves 4**

An unexpected twist on traditional potato salad. I know, going wild, right? Somebody hold us back before it's too late.

1 small yellow onion, sliced

2 tablespoons olive oil

4 large potatoes, cooked, cooled, and chopped

1½ teaspoons cumin

3 tablespoons lemon juice

2 teaspoons Dijon mustard

1 scallion, chopped

¼ teaspoon cayenne pepper

2 tablespoons chopped fresh cilantro

1. In large saucepan, sauté onions in olive oil for 3 minutes.

2. Stir in the chopped potatoes and cumin. Cook for 1 minute and remove from the heat quickly so nothing burns.

3. Whisk together all other ingredients and pour over the potato mixture, stirring well.

4. Chill for an hour and serve!

# Carrot and Date Salad

**Serves 6**

The natural sweetness of carrots and encouraging saccharine flavor of dates meld together perfectly. This salad contains a lot of citrus island flavor! Perfect for a picnic or a day at the beach. Or, to add a little sunshine into your soul.

1 tablespoon olive oil

2 tablespoons agave nectar

3 tablespoons lemon juice

¼ teaspoon salt

4 large carrots, grated

½ cup chopped dates

3 mandarin oranges, sectioned

⅓ cup coconut flakes

1. Mix together olive oil, agave nectar, lemon juice, and salt in a large bowl. Whisk.

2. Add grated carrots and mix well. Stir in dates, oranges, and coconut flakes. Let sit for an hour before serving.

# Tangerine and Mint Salad

**Serves 2**

A simple salad for two that you can throw together when you want something that isn't just your typical greens. Cracked red pepper lends a delicious and soft pepper flavor—as well as a pretty garnish—to this salad. If you can't find any, black works just as well, of course.

1 head green lettuce, chopped

2 tablespoons chopped fresh mint

2 tangerines, sectioned

⅓ cup chopped walnuts

2 tablespoons olive oil

Salt and red pepper to taste

Simply toss together lettuce, mint, tangerines, and walnuts, top with olive oil, and season with salt and pepper.

# CHAPTER 6

# Super Soups

## FOR THOSE LONG, COLD WINTER NIGHTS

Or you know, any time. (I was just trying to be all dramatic. Feel me?)

# Cajun Gumbo

Serves 5

If this doesn't wake up your mouth, I'd call in the EMT. Here we've got such a rich, spicy, fantastic dish that you will be dancing in your kitchen! I am a big fan of spice and this meal surely has my toes tingling and my stomach warm by the time I'm finished eating. Frankly, I feel like switching on some bubbly New Orleans jazz and drinking a tall glass of sweet tea. Don't just stand there, love. There's room for more than one on the floor, and this dish is big enough to serve a family or friends.

1 onion, diced

1 red or green bell pepper, diced

3 stalks celery, chopped

2 tablespoons olive oil

½ teaspoon garlic powder

½ teaspoon salt

¼ teaspoon pepper

1 zucchini, sliced

1 (14-ounce) can diced tomatoes

3 cups vegetable broth

2 teaspoons hot sauce

1 teaspoon file powder (a Creole seasoning made from ground sassafras leaves)

¾ teaspoon thyme

1 teaspoon Cajun seasoning

2 bay leaves

1 (15-ounce) can kidney beans, drained

1½ cups brown rice, cooked

1. In a big stock pot, sauté your onion, bell pepper, and celery for a few minutes in the olive oil. To this sizzling, fragrant mixture, toss in some garlic powder and a little salt and pepper.

2. Lower the heat from high to medium, and add your zucchini, tomatoes, and veggie broth.

3. Add all remaining ingredients and spices except the beans and rice. Simmer, covered, for 30 minutes.

4. Add the beans and cook for another 5 minutes to soften them up and get them to absorb that great broth flavor. Add the rice. If you have more than 1½ cups rice on hand, go ahead and add a little more. Everyone likes rice. Make certain to remove the bay leaves before you eat!

# Chili for Those Who'd Rather Not Cook

Serves 4

I promise this recipe only takes 10 minutes. Cross my heart. Hey, procrastinators need to look out for each other, right? Well, I've got your back. (Tomorrow.) And I've got chili.

1 (12-ounce) jar of salsa (organic always tastes best)

1 (14-ounce) can diced tomatoes, undrained

2 (14-ounce) cans kidney beans or black beans, drained

1½ cups frozen veggies of your choice

4 veggie burgers, crumbled (black bean work great)

2 tablespoons chili powder

1 teaspoon cumin

½ cup water

Salt and pepper to taste

Take a big ol' stock pot and combine everything in it. Get the mixture simmering over medium-high heat for about ten minutes and ay caramba, you're done. And you'll soon be full, too! Thank you, fiber and protein.

# Winter Seitan Stew

Serves 4

A satisfying stew with the big stew flavor. Something for those chilly evenings when you just want to make some comfort food. This dish boasts a "meaty" flavor that will recall beef stews you've had in the past.

2 cups chopped seitan

1 onion, chopped

2 carrots, chopped

2 stalks celery, chopped

2 tablespoons olive oil

4 cups vegetable broth

2 potatoes, chopped

½ teaspoon sage

½ teaspoon rosemary

½ teaspoon thyme

2 tablespoons cornstarch

⅓ cup water

Salt and pepper to taste

1. In a large stock pot on medium-high heat, cook the seitan, onion, carrots, and celery in the olive oil for about 5 minutes. You're going to want to brown the seitan a little bit as you stir.

2. Add the veggie broth to the mix. Add the potatoes and sage, rosemary, and thyme, and let the broth simmer, covering and cooking for 25 minutes.

3. While this is cooking, be all swift and mix the cornstarch and water together in a small bowl. Add this to the pot as well, stirring to mix. Let the broth thicken.

4. Cook uncovered for 7 minutes, season with salt and pepper, and eat up!

# Garlic Miso and Onion Soup

Serves 4

An easy Asian-inspired soup with tofu to fill you up. Plain tofu can sometimes be kind of bland and dull (sorry tofu, but it's true). In this recipe, however, the reliable neutral taste of tofu plays well against the miso and garlic. Hooray for an old vegan staple!

5 cups water

½ cup sliced shiitake mushrooms

3 scallions, chopped

½ onion, chopped

4 cloves garlic, minced

¾ teaspoon garlic powder

2 tablespoons soy sauce

1 teaspoon sesame oil

1 pound block silken tofu, diced

⅓ cup miso

1. Combine all ingredients except miso in a stock pot set on medium-high heat and bring to a simmer, cooking for 12 minutes.

2. Add the miso. Simmer (do not boil!), stirring, for 5 minutes until miso is dissolved all the way through. And you're finished! How simple was that?

# White Bean and Orzo Minestrone

Serves 6

I feel as if this recipe should be stapled onto my heart. Otherwise, my Italian grandmother would smack my poor little head. Alas, I do not want to staple anything to my arteries so I shall write it down here. Happy, Nunna?

3 cloves garlic, minced

1 onion, chopped

2 ribs celery, chopped

2 tablespoons olive oil

5 cups vegetable broth

1 carrot, diced

1 cup green beans, chopped

2 small potatoes, chopped small

2 tomatoes, chopped

1 (15-ounce) can cannellini beans, drained

1 teaspoon basil

½ teaspoon oregano

¼ cup orzo

Salt and pepper to taste

1.  Over medium-high heat, combine garlic, onion, and celery with olive oil in a stock pot. Cook for about 3 minutes, stirring frequently.

2.  Add in veggie broth, carrots, green beans, potatoes, tomatoes, beans, basil, and oregano. Bring to a simmer. Cover and cook on medium for 25 minutes.

3.  Add the orzo in last, and cook for another 10 minutes. Season with salt and pepper. Enjoy with some garlic bread!

# Indian Curried Lentil Soup

Serves 4

One of the most amazing and perfect cuisines for vegetarians is Indian. The country with the largest number of vegetarians in the world is bound to have at least a few specialties, right? So here it is: Indian food made simple. This dish is perfect with a side of warm vegan naan to dip and a silky coconut smoothie to wash it all down.

1 onion, diced

1 carrot, sliced

2 whole cloves

2 tablespoons vegan margarine

1 teaspoon turmeric

1 teaspoon cumin

1 cup yellow or green lentils, uncooked

2¾ cups vegetable broth

2 large tomatoes, chopped

1 teaspoon salt

1 teaspoon lemon juice

¼ teaspoon black pepper

1. In a big stock pot on high heat, brown the onion for about 3 minutes in the vegan margarine. Toss in the carrot and cloves, letting them absorb the flavor.

2. Add the turmeric and cumin, toasting them for 2 minutes. Remember to keep stirring this one! You don't want anything to stick. You might cry. I do.

3. Lower the heat to medium-low, adding all ingredients aside from the lemon juice and black pepper. Simmer, covered, for 45 minutes. Check lentils to make sure they're all cooked before you take the soup off the heat.

4. Season with lemon juice and black pepper. Serve.

# Barley Vegetable Soup

Serves 6

A great veggie soup with a hearty, a typical grain to fill you up. I think this delicious broth goes well with a really crunchy baguette and some fresh pesto. It's the perfect appetizer.

1 onion, chopped

2 carrots, sliced

2 ribs celery, chopped

2 tablespoons olive oil

8 cups vegetable broth

1 cup barley, uncooked

1½ cups frozen broccoli

1 (14-ounce) can crushed tomatoes

½ teaspoon parsley

½ teaspoon thyme

2 bay leaves

Salt and pepper to taste

1. In a big stock pot over high heat, first sauté the onions, carrots, and celery in the olive oil. Let the onions become translucent. This should take approximately 2 minutes. Let's not be hasty.

2. Lower the heat to medium, adding all other ingredients, save the salt and pepper. Simmer, covered, for 45 minutes.

3. Remove the cover and allow to cook uncovered for another 10 minutes. Now you can add the salt and pepper, and then you're done! Don't forget to remove the bay leaves before you chow down.

# Cannellini Bean and Corn Chowder

Serves 4

Never fear, chowder is here. And so is the end of horrible, overused phrases! I promise
. . . tomorrow. Anyway, some folks might lament the loss of corn chowder when they
become vegan, but not you, you clever devil. You've found this recipe and you're smart
as a whip. No mourning for you. Unless of course we're talking about mourning your
previously conceived notion that you can't have creamy, awesome goodness as an
occasional vegan.

1 potato, chopped in small pieces

1 onion, chopped

2 tablespoons olive oil

3 cups vegetable broth

1 tablespoon whole wheat flour

1½ cups soy milk

2 ears of corn, kernels cut off or 1
(16-ounce) bag frozen corn

1 (14-ounce) can cannelloni beans

½ teaspoon thyme

¼ teaspoon black pepper

1. In a stock pot sauté the potato and
   onion in the olive oil on high heat
   until cooked. Go for about 5 minutes.

2. Set heat to medium-low and add the
   veggie broth, letting cook, covered,
   for another 20 minutes.

3. In a separate bowl, whisk the flour
   and soy milk together until smooth.
   Add to the stock pot.

4. Add the corn, beans, thyme, and
   pepper.

5. Cook for about 5 more minutes, stirring frequently and reducing heat just
   a bit. Chow down, on this chow-der!

# Spicy Roasted Tomato Soup

## Serves 4

This warm and zesty soup is perfect for a fall day. Combining the natural sweetness of tomatoes with the spice of cayenne is a perfect pick-me-up. The key to this recipe is finding the freshest ingredients you can. The tastes will be bright and soothing. Just don't get too excited now. You haven't even started cooking yet!

6 large tomatoes (plum tomatoes work great, but if you use them, use 12 rather than 6)

1 small onion

4 cloves garlic

2 tablespoons olive oil

1 teaspoon cayenne pepper

¼ teaspoon black pepper

¼ teaspoon cumin

¾ teaspoon salt

Pinch nutmeg

1¼ cups soy milk

2 tablespoons fresh, chopped basil

1½ teaspoons balsamic vinegar

Splash of red wine

1. Preheat oven to 450°F.

2. Chop tomatoes and onion and then spread them on a baking sheet alongside the garlic. Drizzle with olive oil and sprinkle with both peppers, cumin, salt, and nutmeg. Bake for about an hour.

3. Blend seasoned tomatoes and all remaining ingredients in the food processor. Then heat over the stove in a medium saucepan on high heat for about 2 minutes.

# Not-Chicken Soup

**Serves 6**

Just as comforting and soulful as the real thing. When you've got the sniffles, muster up the energy to cook up a pot of this. Then shuffle back to your bed, encase yourself in your comfiest comforter, put on a terrible TV show, and eat yourself back to health.

6 cups vegetable broth

1 carrot, diced

2 ribs celery, diced

1 yellow onion, chopped

1 vegan "chicken"-flavored bouillon cube

2 bay leaves

1½ teaspoons Italian seasoning

Salt and pepper to taste

1 tablespoon nutritional yeast

1 cup brown rice, cooked

2 teaspoons chili powder (optional)

Combine all ingredients in a pot, and let simmer on low for a good 30 minutes. See? Easy—because you're sick and I love you.

## THE SKINNY ON ... Vegan-Style Meat Flavorings

Sometimes you get tired of veggie broth and want to mix it up—I get it! Believe it or not, there are many brands of "beef" or "chicken"-flavor vegan bouillon cubes. These faux-meat flavorings can be found at places like Whole Foods, and are usually composed of a compressed mixture of yeasts, palm oil, herbs, dried veggies, and spices.

## Potato and Leek Soup

**PROTEIN FIBER**

**Serves 6**

Feeling like you just want to curl up in a dark yet homey mansion nestled somewhere in the country estates of Surrey? Well, you probably can't, but you *can* make this classic English comfort soup. And what better way to console your shattered dreams than food? In all senses of the word, this soup will *root* you warmly into a pleasant, restful mood.

1 yellow onion, diced

2 cloves garlic, minced

2 tablespoons olive oil

6 cups vegetable broth

3 leeks, sliced

2 large potatoes, sliced

2 bay leaves

1 cup soy milk

2 tablespoons vegan margarine

¾ teaspoon salt

⅓ teaspoon black pepper

½ teaspoon sage

½ teaspoon thyme

2 tablespoons nutritional yeast

1.  In a large stock pot sauté onion and garlic in the olive oil on high heat for about 3 minutes.

2.  Add the veggie broth, leeks, potatoes, and bay leaves, bringing to a simmer. Bring heat down to medium and cook for about 30 minutes till the potatoes are done.

3.  Remove the bay leaves. Purée potato-leek mixture in a food processor. Return the purée to the stock pot on the stovetop and add the remaining ingredients. Cook for another 3 minutes on medium-high.

## Shiitake and Garlic Broth

**PROTEIN FIBER**

**Makes 6 cups**

Do you ever try something once and then love it so much you go back and eat it every night for a month? This is one of those dishes. There's no getting out of it. We're in deep shiitake, friends.

⅓ cup dried shiitake mushrooms

6 cups water

2 cloves garlic, smashed

1 bay leaf

½ teaspoon thyme

½ onion, chopped

1.  Combine all ingredients in a large pot and bring to a simmer slowly. Then simply cook for about 40 minutes.

2.  Strain out your veggies before using the stock in another soup, or eating alone as a hot snack.

# CHAPTER 7

# Vegetable Dishes

## FOR THE MOTIVATIONALLY DISINCLINED

Here's a bunch of easy veggie sides that you could very well eat as an entire meal. Just scratch those pesky "serving sizes" from 4 to 1, and eat the whole yield yourself.

# Roasted-Garlic Mashed Taters

Serves 4

There is nothing in the world more comforting than mashed potatoes. Leave the skin on the potatoes—that's where all the nutrients live. The garlic and olive oil in the recipe will keep everything moist, while the soy creamer and nutritional yeast will ensure the creamy flavor that you crave.

1 head of garlic

2 tablespoons olive oil

6 potatoes, cooked

½ cup vegan margarine

½ cup soy creamer

2 teaspoons rosemary

2 tablespoons nutritional yeast

Salt and pepper to taste

1. Preheat oven to 400°F.

2. Remove the outer shell on the head of garlic. Drizzle generously with olive oil and then cover with aluminum foil. Bake for about 30 minutes.

3. Press cloves out of their skins and mash them up with a fork. I feel like we're on the operating table here.

4. Combine all remaining ingredients, including the mashed garlic, in a bowl and season with salt and pepper. *Voila.*

# Sesame Soy Asparagus and Mushrooms

Serves 4

The flavor of sesame is nutty and sweet, and mushrooms lend this dish an earthy flavor that is picked up by the bright notes in the asparagus. This makes a great side to any meal. And it can be colorful too: asparagus comes in white, green, and even purple! (I wish I could be purple.)

1 pound fresh asparagus, trimmed and chopped

¾ cup chopped mushrooms

2 teaspoons sesame oil

1 teaspoon soy sauce

½ teaspoon sugar

½ teaspoon white pepper

2 tablespoons sesame seeds

1. Preheat oven to 350°F.

2. Place asparagus and mushrooms in a baking dish. Roast in the oven for about 10 minutes.

3. Remove from the oven and drizzle with oil and soy sauce. Then sprinkle with sugar and pepper. Toss. Return to the oven for about 6 minutes.

4. Roll the veggies in sesame seeds and serve.

# Gingered and Pralined Sweet Potatoes

Serves 4

Candied sweetness for your favorite holidays. There are vegan marshmallows available in some chain food stores, but you really don't need them for this recipe. Top with a little bit of vegan brown sugar and you're all set.

4 sweet potatoes, baked

¼ cup soy creamer

¼ cup orange juice

½ teaspoon salt

½ cup chopped pecans

2 tablespoons vegan margarine

⅓ cup maple syrup

½ cup whole wheat flour

½ cup candied ginger

½ cup rolled oats

Brown sugar for sprinkling

1. Preheat oven to 350°F.

2. Mash together sweet potatoes, soy creamer, OJ, and salt. Put in an 8"x13" casserole dish.

3. Combine remaining ingredients in a separate bowl and then spread them on top of the sweet potato mixture.

4. Bake for 30 minutes, and you're done, done, done.

**THE** SKINNY **ON . . . Sugar**

Many sugars are bleached using bone char—this includes brown sugars, too! Brown sugars are commonly flavored with molasses, which is what gives it the distinctive tang. In order to make certain your sugar is vegan, check with the manufacturer. A common company that *does* use bone char is Domino. Pillsbury *does not.*

# Cranberry Apple Stuffing

Serves 6

Missing autumn? The pumpkins? The cornstalks? The apple pies loaded with goodness and ice cream? This stuffing will satisfy all those urges and hearken back those spicy cinnamon and clove aromas that you fall in love with every time the leaves change. Enjoy this with some hot mulled cider (or you know, just stick some apple juice in the microwave with cinnamon and nutmeg).

2 tablespoons vegan margarine

1 yellow onion, diced

⅔ cup mushrooms

¾ teaspoon sage

¾ teaspoon thyme

½ teaspoon marjoram

12 slices whole wheat bread, cubed

1 cup dried cranberries

1 apple, diced

½ cup apple juice

2 cups veggie broth

Salt and pepper to taste

1. Preheat oven to 350°F.

2. In a large saucepan on low heat, melt margarine. Add the onion and mushrooms, letting them cook until they're soft.

3. Add the sage, thyme, and marjoram and heat for about another 2 minutes.

4. Stir in the remaining ingredients, mixing thoroughly. Place in a casserole pan and bake for 30 minutes.

# Saucy Indian Veggies

Serves 4

Easy Indian food. How, do you ask? Read on and see, darling. This rich-tasting veggie dish also just happens to be low in calories.

1 (28-ounce) can diced tomatoes

2 potatoes, chopped

½ teaspoon chili powder

2 teaspoons curry powder

1½ teaspoons cumin

½ teaspoon turmeric

1 head cauliflower, chopped up

1 carrot, diced or shredded

¾ cup green peas

¾ teaspoon crushed red pepper flakes

¼ teaspoon salt

1. Mix tomatoes, potatoes, chili powder, curry, cumin, and turmeric in a pot and cover. Cook for 10 minutes on medium.

2. Add all other ingredients and cook for another 15 minutes. Make sure the potatoes are soft by the time you're through.

# Garlic and Soy Sauce Green Beans

Serves 4

Works great as a side dish. I eat green beans compulsively as a snack. Remember: fresh green beans are always better than frozen or canned (blah). They're pretty cheap, too, so pick some up next time you're out. They have a crunch that is simply something else when they're left a little al dente.

1 pound fresh chopped green beans, ends trimmed off

2 tablespoons olive oil

½ teaspoon crushed red pepper flakes

4 cloves garlic, minced

1 teaspoon ginger, fresh, minced

3 tablespoons soy sauce

Black pepper to taste

1. Boil green beans for about 3 minutes. Drain and set aside.

2. Heat the olive oil in a pan, tossing in the red pepper flakes, garlic, ginger, and cooked green beans. Cook for about three minutes.

3. Season with soy sauce and black pepper.

# Sweetened Roast Squash

Serves 4

Delicious and autumnal. Reach for this dish in the fall when squash is in season and there is a nip in the air that calls for a heartful, spicy side that'll warm you from your nose to your toes. Serve simply: Cut in half and scoop out to eat.

1 butternut or acorn squash

1 teaspoon sea salt

4 tablespoons orange juice

4 tablespoons maple syrup

Dash nutmeg

Dash cinnamon

1. Preheat oven to 400°F.

2. Cut squash into fourths and discard the seeds. Place squash in a casserole dish. Give each quarter an equal amount of sea salt, OJ, maple syrup, and a gentle sprinkling of nutmeg and cinnamon.

3. Cover with foil and bake for 45 minutes. Enjoy the scent of fall, my little leaflings!

# Baked Sweet Potato Fries

Serves 2

Waaaaaaaaaaay better than French fries. Don't even go there. Sweet, crunchy, and so much tastier. These puppies go great with a side of honey and a sprinkling of cinnamon and sugar. Or just be old school and eat them with a dash of salt and ketchup. Make them spicy by adding some Cajun seasoning, nutritional yeast, or a little cayenne pepper, or eat them dipped in a vegan cheese dip (see Chapter 13 for recipe).

2 large sweet potatoes, sliced thin into fries

2 tablespoons olive oil

¼ teaspoon garlic powder

½ teaspoon paprika

½ teaspoon brown sugar

½ teaspoon chili powder

½ teaspoon salt

1. Preheat oven to 400°F.

2. Spread out fries on a cookie sheet and brush with olive oil on all sides.

3. In a bowl, combine all the spices and sprinkle over fries.

4. Cook for 10 minutes, turning once. Eat up!

# Honey Mustard and Balsamic Vinegar Green Beans

**Serves 1**

Green beans are crunchy, satisfying, and delicious. I personally would eat them morning, noon, and night if they would cook themselves. That is the only way many foods could be more perfect. Anyway, enjoy this tangy, satisfying dish as a healthy lunch!

¼ red onion, chopped

½ white onion, chopped

3 cloves garlic, minced

1 tablespoon olive oil

½ pound cooked green beans

½ cup fresh broccoli

½ teaspoon paprika

Salt and pepper to taste

1½ tablespoons honey mustard

⅛ cup balsamic vinegar

1 tablespoon nutritional yeast

1. Sauté onions and garlic in olive oil for about 4 minutes, stirring. Add green beans and broccoli and stir to coat in olive oil.

2. Continue cooking for 1 minute and add paprika, salt, and pepper. Stir. Add honey mustard and balsamic vinegar. Continue stirring and cook for 1 minute.

3. Sprinkle top with nutritional yeast and serve warm.

# Spaghetti Squash Dinner

Serves 2

Veggie pasta is some of the best around. Using a food processor, you can grate car-rots or zucchini into pasta-like shapes, vastly plummeting your caloric intake while still enjoying your favorite macaroni dishes. In this case, you don't have to use anything nature didn't give you herself. Spaghetti squash, when cooked, scrapes out into the shape of noodles! Fascinating stuff.

1 spaghetti squash

2 tablespoons olive oil

Salt to taste

Cracked black pepper to taste

Garlic powder to taste

¼ cup balsamic vinegar

¼ cup red wine

1 yellow tomato, diced

About ½ cup your favorite store-bought marinara sauce

2 tablespoons nutritional yeast

1. Preheat oven to 400°F.

2. Cut the squash in half with a sharp knife. Be careful, Butterfingers. Dis-card seeds.

3. Brush the inside of the squash with olive oil and season generously with salt, pepper, and garlic.

4. Place the squash face down on an ungreased baking sheet. Cook for 45 minutes.

5. In a small bowl, combine vinegar and wine. Add diced tomato and let mari-nate while squash cooks.

6. Remove squash from oven. Let cool for 10 minutes. With a fork, scrape out the insides of the spaghetti squash. Divide into 2 bowls.

7. Pour yellow tomatoes and canned sauce over "spaghetti" and sprinkle top with nutritional yeast. How fancy of you.

# Caramelized Baby Carrots

Serves 4

Sweet and small and itty bitty and so cute you'll want to devour them the second they're finished. Watch. You will.

4 cups baby carrots

Water (just enough to cover carrots)

1 teaspoon lemon juice

2 tablespoons margarine

1 tablespoon maple syrup

2 tablespoons vegan brown sugar

½ teaspoon sea salt

1. In a large saucepan, simmer carrots in water for about 8 minutes until soft and cooked through. Drain them, and drizzle the lemon juice over them. They'll absorb it quite well now that they're no longer raw.

2. Heat the carrots again, adding the margarine, maple syrup, brown sugar, and salt. Cook for about 5 minutes (until they glaze over), and you should be golden! I mean . . . caramelized!

## THE SKINNY ON . . . Salt

Sea salt and table salt have different flavors. Sea salt is made from evaporated sea water and is comprised of sodium chloride, calcium, potassium, and other trace minerals. Table salt is pure sodium chloride. Each can lend a subtly different taste to a dish. For reference, sea salt is typically more expensive than table salt.

# CHAPTER 8

# Be Rice

## TO YOURSELF

Dishes you can make once and then store in order to eat all week. Time friendly and delicious. What more could you ask for?

# Spicy Southern Jambalaya

Serves 6

For a dish that pops, try anything with a lot of syllables in it. This is not a Rule, merely a Suggestion. Pack away the rest for leftovers. I always find that making a big rice dish and then eating it throughout the week saves time and hassle. Plus this one will jump-start your taste buds, you Saucy Minx.

2 tablespoons olive oil

1 yellow bell pepper, chopped

1 onion, chopped

1 (14-ounce) can diced tomatoes, undrained

3 cups vegetable broth

2 cups brown or wild rice

1 bay leaf

1 teaspoon paprika

½ teaspoon thyme

½ teaspoon oregano

½ teaspoon garlic powder

1 cup corn, fresh

½ teaspoon cayenne pepper

Splash of hot sauce

1. In a large stock pot on medium heat, heat olive oil. Add bell pepper and cook for 1 minute. Then add onion and cook for another 3 minutes until soft.

2. Reduce heat from medium-high to low, and add remaining ingredients except the cayenne pepper and hot sauce. I know, I know you want to, but don't get too wild on me. Simmer, covered, for 20 minutes.

3. Now add the cayenne and hot sauce. Mix through and through. Let the spice settle in for about 3 minutes and take off the heat. Remove the bay leaf and admire your work.

## PART-TIME TIP

I always use brown rice when cooking. It has more fiber than white rice because the bran of the grain remains. Sort of like white and whole wheat flour. If you want a more filling dish, try adding some white or red kidney beans to the recipe during Step 2. You could even try adding tofu or some pieces of a whole grain baguette that you know won't disintegrate as make-shift croutons!. If you decide to add the bread, add it right after taking the Jambalaya off the stove, and serve immediately.

# Cuban Black Beans, Sweet Potatoes, and Rice

Serves 4

My favorite thing about rice is that it lends itself perfectly to citrus flavors and sweetness. You can have a filling meal with a twist: lime, lemon, or even tangerine. Enjoy this dish as a meal or a side, and serve alongside some orange slices, some melon, or some spicy seasoned tempeh. But I'm just here for moral support—I'm pretty sure you're coming up with ideas of your own. I wave a proud flag for you like your mother at your high school track race! (I'm so proud of you, baby!)

3 cloves garlic, minced

½ white onion, chopped

2 tablespoons olive oil

3 *grande* sweet potatoes, chopped small (forgive me, when I make Cuban food I pretend that I can speak Spanish)

2 (15-ounce) cans black beans, drained

¼ cup vegetable broth

2 cups brown rice, cooked

1 tablespoon chili powder

1 teaspoon paprika

1 teaspoon cumin

1 tablespoon lime juice

Splash hot sauce

1. You know this part by now. In a large pot set on medium-high, sauté the garlic and onion in the olive oil for about 3 minutes. You're like a new puppy, learning so fast. I tend to do the same . . . when it involves eating.

2. Lower the heat to medium-low. Add all other ingredients except the lime juice and hot sauce. Simmer, covered, for 25 minutes.

3. Add in the lime and hot sauce and serve while still all warm and steamy.

# Spanish Artichoke and Zucchini Paella

Serves 4

What is *paella*, you ask? I'll save you the Wikipedia run. It's a traditional Spanish rice dish, served as a main course, that originated in the Valencian province of Espana. It's good. You'll enjoy it. This take on Spain's beloved favorite has turmeric in it rather than saffron because that stuff is expensive. But if you have the purse strings to purchase that most hoity-toity of spices, by all means go for it.

3 cloves garlic, minced

1 yellow onion, minced

2 tablespoons olive oil

1 cup white rice, uncooked

1 (15-ounce) can crushed tomatoes

1 green bell pepper, chopped

1 red or yellow bell pepper, chopped

½ cup canned artichoke hearts, chopped and drained

2 zucchini, sliced

2 cups vegetable broth

1 tablespoon paprika

½ teaspoon turmeric

¼ teaspoon parsley

½ teaspoon salt

1. Cook garlic and onions in olive oil for about 4 minutes in a large skillet over medium-high heat. Add the rice and keep stirring so that nothing sticks or burns. (Burning sucks. Both when cooking rice and at the beach.) Heat rice for one minute.

2. Add all other ingredients, stirring to get everything mixed in evenly. Lower heat, cover, and let simmer for 20 minutes.

## THE SKINNY ON ... Garlic

Did you know garlic is known to have antiviral and antibacterial properties? Garlic contains the amino acid called *allicin*. When consumed raw, allicin breaks up the party called *biosynthesis* in the formation of cell walls, helping to destroy harmful bacteria. Consuming fresh garlic could be good for your health! Pretty cool. Next time you hate on garlic for making your breath smell like death, remember garlic has feelings too, and also just might ward off that nasty cold.

# Chinese Fried Rice with Tofu and Cashews

**Serves 3**

Chinese food is incredible for its mastery of mixing both savory and sweet flavors. This recipe takes plain old boiled white rice (which you can make and store all week) and turns it into something delicious.

2 cloves garlic, minced

1 (12-ounce) block tofu, mashed with a fork or cut into cubes

3 tablespoons olive oil, divided

3 cups rice, cooked

½ cup fresh or frozen mixed, cut veggies

3 tablespoons soy sauce

1 tablespoon sesame oil

¼ teaspoon sugar

¼ cup unsweetened smooth peanut butter

2 tablespoons lime juice

3 scallions, diced

⅓ cup chopped cashews

1. In a large skillet, sauté the garlic and tofu in 2 tablespoons of the olive oil for about 8 minutes. Make sure the tofu is browned. Medium-high heat should do it.

2. Add rice, veggies, and the remaining 1 tablespoon of olive oil. Stir well.

3. Add soy sauce, sesame oil, sugar, and peanut butter. Stir constantly, allowing everything to cook for a good 4 minutes.

4. Then, take off the heat and add lime juice, scallions, and cashews.

# Bellissimo Italian Rice Salad

Serves 4

The flavors of Italy are decadent and rich. The sweet smell of tomato sauce and the savory flavors of cheese recall the romantic serenade of the accordion over dinner by candlelight. Luckily, you can recreate these taste-memories is a very vegan way.

1 tablespoon balsamic vinegar

⅓ cup red wine vinegar

2 teaspoons Dijon mustard

4 cloves garlic, minced

1 teaspoon basil

⅓ cup chopped, fresh parsley

½ cup olive oil

2 cups brown rice, cooked

1 (14-ounce) can diced tomatoes

1 carrot, grated

½ cup roasted red peppers, chopped

½ cup green olives, sliced

¼ cup nutritional yeast (optional)

Salt and pepper to taste

1. In a small bowl, whisk together balsamic vinegar, red wine vinegar, Dijon mustard, garlic, basil, parsley, and olive oil.

2. In a large bowl, mix rice and other ingredients together. Add the balsamic mixture. Stir well.

3. Chill in the fridge for 30 minutes before serving.

# Greek Lemon Rice with Spinach

Serves 4

A light, zesty recipe, reminiscent of the Greek dish *spanakorizo*. Go on, fair Hestia, impress me.

1 onion, chopped

4 cloves garlic, minced

2 tablespoons olive oil

¾ cup rice, uncooked

2½ cups vegetable broth

1 (8-ounce) can tomato paste

2 bunches fresh spinach, trimmed

2 tablespoons chopped, fresh parsley

1 tablespoon fresh mint

2 tablespoons lemon juice

½ teaspoon salt

½ teaspoon ground black pepper

1. In a large skillet on medium-high, sauté onion and garlic in olive oil for about 2 minutes. Add the rice and brown lightly, making certain to stir occasionally, about 2 minutes longer.

2. Add the broth, cover, and cook for 12 minutes.

3. Add the tomato paste, spinach, and parsley to the rice, and cook for 5 more minutes. Cover again while cooking.

4. Stir in all remaining ingredients. Take off heat and serve warm!

# Curried Rice and Lentils

Serves 4

This recipe is delicious with a little tempeh thrown in. Try adding some chick peas for extra protein and sopping up scoops of it with whole wheat vegan naan.

1½ cups brown rice

1 cup red or brown lentils

3½ cups vegetable broth

1 bay leaf

1 tablespoon curry powder

½ teaspoon cumin

½ teaspoon turmeric

½ teaspoon garlic powder

Salt and pepper to taste

Hot sauce (optional)

Combine all the ingredients except salt, pepper, and hot sauce in a large pot. Simmer, covered, for 20 minutes. Then season with salt and pepper. Maybe even add a dash of hot sauce for an unexpected twist.

## THE SKINNY ON . . . Naan

Naan is a traditional Indian bread. Fluffy and light, it is served warm and is a staple for most Indian dinners. Traditional naan (that you find in restaurants or at the store) are usually made with milk and butter, as well as egg. All no's for us vegans! Luckily, you can substitute any naan recipe ingredient-for-ingredient with soy milk, vegan margarine, and egg-replacer!

# Caribbean Red Beans and Rice

Serves 4

A complete classic. If you have it around, toss in some vegan bacon or ham.

3 cloves garlic, crushed

1 small onion, chopped

2 tablespoons olive oil

2 tablespoons fresh chopped parsley

½ teaspoon rosemary

½ teaspoon thyme

¼ teaspoon cloves

1 (15-ounce) can kidney beans

3 cups vegetable broth

2 bay leaves

1½ cups rice, uncooked

Salt and pepper to taste

1. In a large saucepan over medium-high heat, sauté onion and garlic in olive oil until soft. In about 4 minutes, add the parsley, rosemary, thyme, and cloves, and continue cooking while stirring.

2. Add the beans, stirring until coated in oil. Cook well for about 2 minutes, stirring continually.

3. Add all other ingredients except salt and pepper. Reduce heat to a simmer, cover, and cook for 30 minutes.

4. Uncover, and let cook for another 10 minutes until liquid is absorbed. Season with salt and pepper. Remember to take out the bay leaves before eating.

## PART-TIME TIP

Cooking with dried beans is often much less expensive than canned. Cooking your own takes up a little time, but it also allows you to control how much sodium you get in your serving of legumes. Canned beans are often surreptitiously filled with salt, gumshoe. Approximately ⅔ cup dried beans equals 1 (15-ounce) can of canned beans.

# Hawaiian Pineapple and Mint Rice

Serves 6

Have a little cabin fever? Try a little island fever. This rice dish is refreshing and sweet—something that will cool you off on a hot day. So close your eyes, take a bite, and imagine you're on an island holiday, surrounded by the lapping waves of the Pacific. Let this dish help you say Aloha to reality, because reality is so dull. Pineapple rice is better.

4 cups white rice, cooked

½ cup chopped macadamia or cashew nuts

1 cup diced pineapple (fresh if available)

½ cup raisins

¼ cup dried papaya

⅓ cup pineapple juice

2 tablespoons olive or safflower oil

2 tablespoons red wine vinegar

¼ cup toasted coconut flakes

2 tablespoons chopped mint

1. Mix rice, nuts, pineapple, raisins, and papaya in a large bowl. Set aside.

2. In a different bowl, whisk the pineapple juice, oil, and vinegar. Add to the rice mixture. Chill for 1½ hours.

3. Only add coconut flakes and mint right before serving so they don't get soggy and sad looking.

# Cranberry Apple Wild Rice

Serves 4

A delicious mix of sweet and salty, this recipe can be reworked as a great breakfast dish. Just replace the vegetable broth with almond or soy milk; the salt and pepper with brown sugar and cinnamon; the olive oil with honey; and the scallions, onions, and celery with raisins.

1 red onion, diced

2 tablespoons olive oil

1 cup wild rice

3 cups vegetable broth

⅓ cup orange juice

½ cup dried cranberries

½ cup pine nuts or almonds

2 scallions, chopped

1 apple, diced

Salt and pepper to taste

1. In a large saucepan on medium-high, sauté onion in olive oil for about 3 minutes.

2. Reduce heat to low. Add rice and vegetable broth. Simmer, covered, for 30 minutes. Add orange juice and simmer, covered, for another 15 minutes.

3. Remove from stove, add cranberries, and let sit for 5 minutes. Toss in all other ingredients and serve.

# CHAPTER 9

# Pasta Dishes

## (BRING YOUR OWN ACCORDION AND CANDLE)

You won't break a sweat with these, and you'll also be convinced of your culinary prowess. Pride! Bad for the Roman Caesars, good for us. (Sorry, Julius.)

# Artichoke and Spinach Pesto Pasta

Serves 4

The tartness of artichokes and leafy freshness from pesto make this a succulent and filling dish packed with the nutritional benefits of spinach and the good monosaturated fats of walnuts. Super brain food for a super human like you!

1 cup fresh basil

1 cup spinach leaves

3 cloves garlic

½ cup walnuts

1 tablespoon lemon juice

2 tablespoons nutritional yeast

½ teaspoon salt

½ teaspoon pepper

2 tablespoons olive oil

1 cup chopped artichoke hearts

2 tablespoons vegan margarine

1 tablespoon flour

¾ cup soy milk

2 cups whole wheat pasta, cooked

1 avocado, diced

1. In a food processor, process the basil, spinach, garlic, walnuts, lemon juice, nutritional yeast, salt, and pepper. Stop when the mixture is almost smooth. Then add the olive oil and artichoke hearts, continuing to process until artichokes are diced very small. Set aside.

2. In a small saucepan, melt the margarine over medium-low heat and add the flour, followed by the soy milk. Cook until thick and paste-like.

3. Combine the basil mixture with the margarine mixture. Then toss with pasta and diced avocados. Serve warm.

# Eggplant Puttanesca

Serves 4

Eggplant holds any flavor well, which works perfectly for tangy puttanesca sauce. Try using this sauce, including the eggplant, on top of pasta, or on a pizza crust sans the capers. Their intense flavor can be a little too strong for a small slice of pizza.

2 tablespoons olive oil

1 red bell pepper, chopped

1 eggplant, chopped

3 cloves garlic, minced

2 tablespoons capers

⅓ cup sliced kalamata olives

½ teaspoon red pepper flakes

1 (14-ounce) can diced tomatoes

1 tablespoon balsamic vinegar

½ teaspoon parsley

1. In a large saucepan, heat olive oil. Sauté bell pepper and eggplant for 4–5 minutes over medium-high heat. Add the garlic and sauté for an additional 2 minutes. Add capers, olives, and red pepper flakes and stir continuously for about 1 minute.

2. Reduce heat to low, adding all other ingredients and allowing to simmer. Cover and continue simmering for 12 minutes. Serve over pasta.

# Gnocchi and Walnut Parsley Sauce

## Serves 4

Gnocchi is a delicious, chewy pasta made from potatoes. Being a root earth vegetable, potato pairs well with rich and savory sauces. Here, walnuts lend a smooth and maple-like flavor, while parsley adds some herbal high notes. It sounds like we are conducting a symphony! Of food! How marvelous.

1 cup chopped walnuts

2½ cups soy milk

2 tablespoons vegan margarine

2 tablespoons all-purpose flour

½ teaspoon parsley, dried

2 teaspoons nutritional yeast

½ teaspoon salt

¼ teaspoon black pepper

1 package gnocchi, cooked (check to make sure it's vegan, lots of gnocchi brands use egg)

1.  In a large saucepan on low heat, cook walnuts in soy milk for approximately 5 minutes. This will soften the nuts. Remove from heat and set aside.

2.  In another large saucepan, heat margarine and flour on medium-low heat. Stir constantly.

3.  Very slowly, whisk in the walnut mixture. Stir continuously for about 5 minutes. The sauce will thicken.

4.  Remove from the heat. Add in parsley, nutritional yeast, salt, and pepper. Serve over cooked gnocchi.

## PART-TIME TIP

When cooking with any non-dairy milk, it's always best to stick to unsweetened varieties when you're not making dessert. You don't want your pasta sauce to taste like vanilla and sugar, do you? (Or maybe you do. I don't know. That's weird.)

# Creamy Sun-Dried Tomato Pasta

**Serves 6**

A sweet and rich sauce that happens to be low in fat. How'd that happen? It's vegan, that's how.

1 pound block silken tofu, drained

¼ cup soy milk

2 tablespoons red wine vinegar

½ teaspoon minced garlic from a jar

½ teaspoon sugar

½ teaspoon salt

1¼ cup sun-dried tomatoes, dehydrated (buy the ones stored in oil)

1 teaspoon dried parsley

1 (12-ounce) package whole wheat pasta, cooked

2 tablespoons chopped fresh basil

1. Process all ingredients, except basil and pasta, in the food processor until very smooth.

2. Transfer mixture to saucepan and heat on low until very hot.

3. Pour over cooked pasta, sprinkling with chopped basil, and dig in!

# Pumpkin Cream Pasta

Serves 4

This sauce, which tastes so richly of autumn, also makes a great dipping sauce for hot garlic breadsticks. You'll be smiling like a Jack O' Lantern by the time you're through.

1 yellow onion, chopped

2 cloves garlic, minced

2 tablespoons vegan margarine

1½ cups soy cream

1 (15-ounce) can puréed pumpkin

½ cup nutritional yeast

½ teaspoon parsley

Salt and pepper to taste

2 cups whole wheat pasta, cooked

1. In a large saucepan over medium-high heat, melt the vegan margarine. Then cook onion and garlic for about 4 minutes.

2. Lower heat to medium. Add the soy cream and pumpkin, stirring and bringing to a simmer. Cook for ten minutes, stirring frequently to ensure that ingredients blend smoothly.

3. Add all other ingredients except pasta, letting cook for another 2 minutes. Pour over whole wheat pasta and serve.

# Lemon, Basil, and Artichoke Pasta

Serves 4

All of these main ingredients have sharp, bright flavors that will treat the tongue right. Try eating this sauce with bowtie pasta and a side of roasted red potatoes.

12 ounces pasta, cooked

1 (6-ounce) jar of artichoke hearts, drained and chopped

2 large tomatoes, chopped

½ cup fresh chopped basil

½ cup sliced black olives

2 tablespoons olive oil

1 tablespoon lemon juice

½ teaspoon rosemary

2 tablespoons nutritional yeast

Salt and pepper to taste

In a large saucepan on low heat, mix cooked pasta with all other ingredients. Heat well, stirring continuously, for about 4 minutes.

# Five-Minute Vegan Pasta Salad

Serves 4

Easy to make, easier to eat. For those lazy days. Even the description is short.

4 cups pasta, cooked

¼ cup Italian salad dressing (look at the label to make sure it's vegan)

3 scallions, chopped

½ cup sliced black olives

½ cup roasted red peppers

1 (14-ounce) can chick peas, drained and rinsed

1 tomato, chopped

1 avocado, diced

Salt and pepper to taste

Simply toss together all ingredients. Store in fridge for a good hour before serving.

## PART-TIME TIP

Basically, cook some pasta and toss in whatever you have on hand. Lemon juice? Great. Black beans? Perfect. Canned corn? Basil? Green beans? Pasta sauce? Add whatever you can think of with a small splash of vinegar or your favorite dressing. Just chill in the fridge for a simple pasta salad, or serve warm right after cooking pasta!

# Sweet and Spicy Peanut Noodles

Serves 4

Such a delicious, dual-natured recipe. Deceptively sweet and then bitingly spicy. The mixture of peanut butter and sesame oil gives this recipe such an exotic flavor, you'll be revisiting Asia again and again.

1 (12-ounce) package Asian-style Udon or soba noodles

⅓ cup natural chunky peanut butter (unsweetened)

3 tablespoons soy sauce

⅔ cup pineapple juice, bottled

2 cloves garlic, minced

1 teaspoon freshly ground ginger, grated

½ teaspoon salt

2–3 small chilies, minced

⅔ cup diced pineapple

1 tablespoon olive oil

1 teaspoon sesame oil

1. Prepare noodles as instructed on their package and set aside.

2. In a medium saucepan over low heat, cook the peanut butter, soy sauce, pineapple juice, garlic, ginger, and salt. Stir until everything is combined.

3. In a large saucepan, heat the minced chilies and diced pineapple in the olive oil and the sesame oil. Cook until pineapple has browned a bit. Add the noodles and stir frequently for about 2 minutes.

4. Reduce heat to low and add the peanut sauce, stirring everything together and cooking for another 2 minutes. I don't need to read from your fortune cookie to know you're going to love this.

# Tofu Lasagna

Serves 4

But how can you have lasagna without ricotta? My Italian grandmother would woefully shake her hands at me, and then probably disown me. But hey, no one said veganism was gonna make you any friends! And it is delicious. Friends aren't delicious. (At least, I don't think so.)

1 pound firm block tofu

1 (12-ounce) block silken tofu

½ cup nutritional yeast

1 tablespoon lemon juice

1 tablespoon soy sauce

1 teaspoon garlic powder

2 teaspoons basil

3 tablespoons chopped fresh parsley

1 teaspoon salt

4 cups spaghetti sauce

1 (16-ounce) pack of lasagna noodles, cooked

1 (8-ounce) package shredded vegan cheese (Daiya brand is awesome and comes in mozzarella flavor)

1. Preheat oven to 350°F.

2. In a medium bowl, mash together the two tofus, nutritional yeast, lemon juice, soy sauce, garlic powder, basil, parsley, and salt until completely ground. Try to make it look like ricotta, yum. Taste it; it'll be good!

3. In a casserole dish, line the bottom with sauce, and then add a layer of noodles. Add a layer of the tofu mixture.

4. Continue layering until everything is used up! Sprinkle top of lasagna with shredded vegan cheese. Cover with aluminum foil and bake for 25 minutes. Try not to build the lasagna over the top of the casserole pan—you don't want any explosions. Explosions aren't fun. Unless, of course, you're an Evil Mastermind. Then go right ahead.

# Asian-Sesame Noodles

Serves 4

Use any kind of pasta you have lying around if you can't make it to the store. Tangy and tasty, here is your fortune: you'll get addicted to this easy-to-make sauce.

1 pound Asian-style rice, Udon, or soba noodles

½ cup tahini

½ cup water

2 tablespoons soy sauce

1 clove garlic

2 teaspoons fresh ginger, minced

2 tablespoons rice vinegar

1 red bell pepper, sliced very thin

2 scallions, chopped

¾ cup snow peas, chopped

2 teaspoons sesame oil

¼ teaspoon crushed red pepper flakes

1. Cook noodles according to package instructions.

2. In a blender, combine tahini, water, soy sauce, garlic, ginger, and rice vinegar.

3. In a large saucepan over medium-high heat, sauté the bell pepper, scallions, and snow peas in the sesame oil for 3 minutes. Add the tahini mixture and the noodles, stirring until completely combined.

4. Cook for 4 more minutes. Garnish with crushed red pepper flakes and serve, grasshopper!

# You Better Believe It: Baked Mac n' Cheese

Serves 6

Dairy-free mac n' cheese for all the vegan-doubters out there. I always say veganism isn't about trying to recreate old favorites as if they're something irreplaceable; it's about creating new favorites from healthy, clean foods. However . . . in this case, we make an exception.

1 (12-ounce) package whole wheat macaroni

1 pound block silken tofu

1 cup almond or soy milk

1 teaspoon tahini

1 tablespoon lemon juice

½ teaspoon apple cider vinegar

1 tablespoon miso

¼ cup nutritional yeast

1 teaspoon garlic powder

1 teaspoon onion powder

1 teaspoon white pepper

2 tablespoons vegan margarine

1 cup whole wheat bread crumbs

½ teaspoon salt

½ teaspoon paprika

½ teaspoon nutmeg

1. Preheat oven to 350°F.

2. Prepare macaroni according to package directions, drain, and place into a casserole dish.

3. Purée the tofu, soy or almond milk, tahini, lemon juice, apple cider vinegar, miso, nutritional yeast, garlic powder, onion powder, and white pepper. Make certain to blend well.

4. Pour "cheese" sauce over the macaroni in the casserole dish.

5. In a small saucepan over medium-high heat, melt the margarine and mix the bread crumbs in, stirring so nothing burns. Spread the bread crumbs over the macaroni.

6. Top the macaroni with salt, paprika, and nutmeg. Feel free to add any other vegan cheese product you might have lying around as a topping, too.

7. Bake for 25 minutes. Eat!

# CHAPTER 10

# Fun with Grains

What do vegan zombies eat? GRAINS!!
(Get it?)

# Lemon Quinoa Veggie Salad

Serves 4

Quinoa is great for any meal because it is so filling. You won't even need seconds. Top up the dish with a plethora of fiberful veggies and the spark of lemon and you've gone all perfect on me.

4 cups vegetable broth

1½ cups quinoa

1 cup fresh broccoli, or frozen broccoli (thawed)

¼ cup lemon juice

¼ cup olive oil

1 teaspoon garlic powder

½ teaspoon salt

¼ teaspoon black pepper

2 tablespoons chopped fresh parsley

1. In a stock pot over high heat, add vegetable broth and quinoa. Bring to a boil and then lower to a simmer and continue cooking on low heat, covered, for 20 minutes. Add broccoli and stir. Quinoa will be finished when all liquid is evaporated from pan.

2. Remove from heat and add other ingredients. Serve, and store leftovers in the fridge—they'll keep for up to 5 days.

# Mediterranean Quinoa Pilaf

**Serves 4**

You don't need to spend a fortune to experience the rich, lively flavors of the Mediterranean coast. Pop open a bottle of red wine and pass around this dish. Remember to share with the whole family in true Italian style.

1½ cups quinoa

3 cups vegetable broth

3 tablespoons balsamic vinegar

1 tablespoon lemon juice

2 tablespoons olive oil

⅓ teaspoon salt

½ cup sun-dried tomatoes, chopped

½ cup artichoke hearts

½ cup kalamata olives, sliced

1. In a stock pot over high heat, add vegetable broth and quinoa. Bring to a boil and then lower to a simmer and continue cooking on low heat, covered, for 20 minutes, until quinoa is cooked through and the liquid is evaporated.

2. Add balsamic vinegar, lemon juice, oil, and salt, and fluff with a fork. Allow to sit for a minute and then add remaining ingredients, stirring well.

## PART-TIME TIP

Have some other Italian ingredients lying around? Toss in some chopped fresh tomato, or some chopped fresh parsley. Add some pepperoncini and red onion for an extra kick!

# Quinoa and Fresh Herb Stuffing

Serves 6

An untraditional turn on a common favorite. This dish is packed full of protein that a typical stuffing would lack. The taste always reminds me of warm evenings stuffed in a cozy cottage in the mountains.

¼ cup vegan margarine

2 ribs celery, diced

1 yellow onion, chopped

1 teaspoon chopped fresh rosemary

2 teaspoons chopped fresh marjoram

1½ teaspoons fresh thyme

1 tablespoon chopped fresh sage

6 slices dry whole wheat bread, cubed

1¼ cups vegetable broth

2 cups cooked quinoa (white or red works best)

¾ teaspoon salt

½ teaspoon pepper

1. Preheat oven to 400°F.

2. In a large saucepan over medium-high heat, melt the margarine. Then cook the celery and onion in it for 8 minutes or until soft. Add the rosemary, marjoram, thyme, and sage and cook for another 3–4 minutes until that good smell permeates the kitchen!

3. Remove from heat. Add the bread and vegetable broth, making sure the bread cubes are moistened.

4. Add the quinoa, salt, and pepper. Put mixture in casserole dish. Cover and bake for 30 minutes.

## THE SKINNY ON . . . Quinoa

Quinoa comes in a variety of colors such as red, white, and black. Black and red quinoas have a "nuttier" flavor and a crunchier texture than white quinoa. White quinoa is most equivalent to your standard pastina pasta.

# Black Bean and Barley Taco Salad

Serves 2 (how romantic)

Craving the rich, tasty, meaty, mouth-watering satisfaction of Mexican? Look no further. Barley adds a satisfying chewy fullness to this meal. *Su corazon ha sido capturado.* Translation: your heart has been captured.

1 (15-ounce) can black beans, drained

½ teaspoon cumin

½ teaspoon oregano

½ teaspoon onion powder

2 tablespoons lime juice

1 teaspoon hot chili sauce

1 cup cooked barley

1 head iceberg lettuce, shredded

1 handful of tortilla chips, crumbled (try the blue corn kind!)

¾ cup natural cold salsa in the refrigerated section (it tastes better, trust me)

2 tablespoons vegan ranch dressing (see Chapter 4 for recipe)

1. In a medium bowl, mash up beans, cumin, oregano, onion powder, lime juice, and hot chili sauce. Squish up as best you can and then add the barley.

2. Layer with lettuce and chips, and top with salsa. Drizzle the ranch dressing over the top.

# Baked Millet Patties

**Makes 8 patties**

Nutty and delicious, wholesome and nutritious. Good for me, good for you, good for . . . okay, I'll stop rhyming. Eat this topped with a whole grain bun and a slice of vegan cheese. There are several varieties available at your local natural foods store. Add some grilled red onions, a little honey mustard and hummus, and there you go.

1½ cups cooked millet

½ cup tahini

1 teaspoon parsley

¾ teaspoon garlic powder

½ teaspoon onion powder

½ teaspoon salt

1.  Preheat oven to 350°F.

2.  Mix all ingredients in a medium bowl, mashing up well. Form into patties and place on a baking sheet.

3.  Cook for about 10 minutes on each side.

### THE SKINNY ON . . . Vegan Cheese

There are several kinds of vegan cheese slices available, lots of them made from ingredients like rice, soy, almond, or vegetables. Most of the time, these options are extremely low in fat as well! They're perfect for grilled cheese or burgers like this. If you're going for strict vegan, you will want to check the label to make certain there is no casein protein (an animal product from milk). There are so many flavors available—mozzarella, cheddar, American, pepper jack—you're certain to find a favorite.

# Black Quinoa with Lime and Rice Vinegar

Serves 4

In the mood for something with a bit of heat and tang? In the mood for something that will take about twenty minutes to prepare because you're lazy like me? Look no further! This succulent side dish works just as well as a main course.

1 cup black (or regular) quinoa

1½ cups water

2½ tablespoons canola oil

1 red bell pepper, chopped

¾ of a whole yellow onion, chopped

¼ teaspoon paprika (optional) for Step 2

¼ teaspoon salt (optional)

½ teaspoon white pepper (optional)

½ teaspoon salt

2 tablespoons lime juice

1 teaspoon cayenne pepper

3 teaspoons rice vinegar

¼ teaspoon paprika for Step 3

1. In a large saucepan over high heat, mix the quinoa and the water. Bring to a boil and then reduce heat to low. Simmer, covered, for approximately 20 minutes. I understand. I always get antsy, too.

2. While the quinoa simmers, heat the canola oil over medium-high heat in a different saucepan. Add the red bell pepper and cook for 5 minutes. Then add the onion, and cook for another 2–3 minutes. (Peppers take longer to cook.) Toss in some extra paprika and a little salt and white pepper to infuse flavor, if you wish.

3. Take the quinoa off the heat and add the peppers and onions.

4. Add the salt, lime, cayenne pepper, rice vinegar, and paprika. Ease up on the cayenne if you can't handle the heat. But I know you can. I know it.

## THE SKINNY ON . . . Frying Oils

Canola, sesame, and coconut oils are the best oils to fry in. This is because their chemical composition resists change at the high temperatures used during fry-cooking! Hooray for science, right? Also, the lack of flavor in canola and coconut oil helps to keep the flavor of the frying items unspoiled.

# Bulgur Wheat Tabbouleh Salad with Tomatoes

Serves 4

A traditional Mediterranean dish that is juicy and full of the taste of fresh parsley and mint. Traditionally a great side dish alongside hummus and falafel.

1¼ cups vegetable broth

1 cup bulgur wheat

3 tablespoons olive oil

¼ cup lemon juice

1 teaspoon garlic powder

½ teaspoon sea salt

½ teaspoon pepper

3 scallions, chopped

½ cup chopped fresh mint

½ cup chopped fresh parsley

3 large tomatoes, chopped

1. In a small saucepan, bring vegetable broth to a boil.

2. Put bulgur in a medium bowl. Pour boiling veggie broth over bulgur. Cover and let sit for 30 minutes.

3. Toss bulgur with olive oil, lemon juice, garlic powder, and salt. Stir this puppy up. Add all other ingredients and fluff the mixture with a fork, adding the tomatoes at the end.

4. Chill for an hour and serve.

# Barley and Mushroom Pilaf

**Serves 4**

What the hell does *pilaf* mean? That's what I thought the first time I heard of one. It's a dish cooked in a rich broth and pungent seasonings. Make certain to buy pearl barley. It cooks in twenty minutes, which makes it my personal favorite.

3 tablespoons vegan margarine, divided

1 cup porcini mushrooms, sliced

1 cup shiitake mushrooms, sliced

2 ribs celery, diced

½ onion, chopped

1¼ cups barley

3¾ cups vegetable broth

1 bay leaf

¼ teaspoon sage

½ teaspoon parsley

½ teaspoon thyme

1. In a large stock pot over medium-high heat, melt 2 tablespoons of margarine. Then sauté both kinds of mushrooms, celery, and onion for 3 minutes. Add barley and remaining 1 tablespoon of margarine. Stir frequently and cook for about 3 more minutes.

2. When barley is toasted and has a brownish tint, add the veggie broth and other spices. Cover and cook for 25 minutes. Stir every now and then, and remember to take out the bay leaf before eating.

# Easy Garlic Quinoa

**Serves 4**

You can never have too much garlic! It has both antiviral and antibacterial properties! (Isn't it fun discussing the immune system?) This is an easy dish to mix up some veggies in, if you so wish.

1 yellow onion, diced

4 cloves garlic, minced

2 tablespoons vegan margarine

3 cups vegetable broth

1½ cups quinoa

½ teaspoon salt

½ teaspoon black pepper

2 tablespoons nutritional yeast

1. Recipe has *easy* in the title for a reason. In a stock pot over medium-high heat sauté onion and garlic in vegan margarine for about 3 minutes. Add veggie broth and quinoa, cover, and let simmer. Cook for 15 minutes.

2. Fluff up when cooked and stir in salt, pepper, and nutritional yeast.

# Lemon Cilantro Couscous

Serves 4

A cheery side dish that is far from heavy. *Couscous* is the cutest word ever, and it is also whole-wheat semolina pasta, rather than a "whole grain" by the books. Eat this dish with some sautéed spinach or roasted squash, eggplant, and red onions. Get its phone number and make it your best friend.

2 cups vegetable broth

1 cup couscous

⅓ cup lemon juice

½ cup chopped fresh cilantro

¼ teaspoon sea salt

1. In a large saucepan over medium-high heat, bring vegetable broth to a simmer. Add couscous and cover. Cook for 10 minutes.

2. When finished, add lemon juice, cilantro, and salt.

# Quinoa Mac n' "Cheese"

## Serves 4

Delicious, full of protein, mixed with veggies, and not a heavy cheese or milk ingredient in sight! You might just ask yourself why you've never done this before. Try this one on your non-vegan friends and dare them to tell you they don't like it. Bet your infant son! Or your grandmother. This one is a winner.

3 cups vegetable broth

1½ cups quinoa

1 onion, chopped

3 cloves garlic, minced

2 tablespoons olive oil

1 bunch broccoli, diced

1 large tomato, diced

1 tablespoon whole wheat flour

¾ cup soy milk

½ teaspoon salt

1 cup shredded vegan cheese

1 cup seasoned bread crumbs

½ teaspoon dried parsley

½ teaspoon nutmeg

1. Preheat oven to 350°F.

2. In a stock pot over high heat, bring vegetable broth to boil and then lower heat so broth is at a simmer on low heat. Add quinoa. Cover and let cook for 20 minutes.

3. In a large saucepan, sauté onion and garlic in the olive oil. Add broccoli and tomato and cook for about 4 minutes.

4. Add flour to the onion mixture, and then add the soy milk and salt. Continue mixing until sauce is thickened, about 3 minutes.

5. In a casserole dish, mix quinoa and onion mixture together. Add the vegan shredded cheese and mix thoroughly. Sprinkle bread crumbs, parsley, and nutmeg over top. Bake 12 minutes.

# Summer Squash and Barley Risotto

Serves 4

When summer is curving into autumn, utilize the last of the bright summer squash while you still can. Ideal for stir fries and an excellent and colorful mix-in for any grain dish, they add a fresh crisp flavor. Adding some porcini mushrooms and asparagus for more variety is also great!

2 cloves garlic, minced

½ onion, diced

1 zucchini, chopped

1 yellow squash, chopped

2 tablespoons olive oil

1 cup pearled barley

3 cups veggie broth

2 tablespoons fresh chopped basil

2 tablespoons vegan margarine

2 tablespoons nutritional yeast

Salt and pepper to taste

## THE SKINNY ON . . . Risotto

Risotto is a dish cooked with a grain (usually rice), and simmer until very rich and creamy. Try using all different types of grains—it's time to experiment! There's bulgur wheat, millet, barley, quinoa, and so many kinds of rice you probably can't wrap your mind around it.

1. In a large saucepan over medium-high heat, sauté the garlic, onion, zucchini, and yellow squash in the olive oil for 4 exciting minutes. Add barley, stirring frequently, and cook for 1 minute until browned and toasted. (I love when things brown. It's so exciting . . . .)

2. Add in 1 cup veggie broth. Let this simmer and cover for about 4 minutes until all liquid is absorbed. Add in 1 more cup of veggie broth and cover and cook for 25 minutes.

3. Cook continually until the barley has become soft. You may need to add in more veggie broth throughout the 25 minutes.

4. When barley is all cooked through, add another ½ cup veggie broth and the basil, stirring until heated.

5. Remove from heat and mix in the margarine, nutritional yeast, and salt and pepper. Serve warm with a light arugula salad or crunchy whole grain cranberry bread.

# Millet and Butternut Squash Casserole

**Serves 4**

I know, I know. Another squash dish! Well, EXCUSE me, okay? I like squash. It is amazing. You shall understand and love this. . . . This is a great autumn dish, after all the summer squashes have waved goodbye for the duration of the cold months.

1 cup millet

2 cups vegetable broth

1 small butternut squash, peeled, seeded, and chopped

½ cup water

1 teaspoon curry powder

½ cup orange juice

½ teaspoon salt

2 tablespoons nutritional yeast

¼ cup chopped almonds

1. In a large saucepan over medium heat, cook millet in veggie broth for 20 minutes. Easy peasy.

2. In another pan, place butternut squash in the water, covering and cooking for 20 minutes. You want the squash to be all soft and cuddly.

3. Yes, I said *cuddly,* okay. Next, mix the millet with the drained squash, on low heat. Add in curry powder and orange juice, stirring to combine. Cook for another 4 minutes.

4. Remove from heat and mix in salt and nutritional yeast. Top with almonds.

# Vegetarian "Beef" and Barley Stew

Serves 4

Before I became a vegetarian many years ago, beef was my favorite meat. Steak, burgers, absolutely anything that tasted like a cow. Poultry, not my bag. Pork, no thanks. And I have never touched fish. So that is why any recipe that has a beefy flavor just does me in. (Don't make that sound dirty in your head!)

1 onion, chopped

2 ribs celery, chopped

1 carrot, chopped

1 green bell pepper, chopped

2 tablespoons olive oil

1 cup water

2½ cups tomato juice

⅓ cup barley

1½ teaspoons chili powder

1½ teaspoons parsley

2 bay leaves

3 veggie burgers, crumbled

Salt and pepper to taste

1. In a large stock pot over medium-high heat, cook the onion, celery, carrot, and pepper in the olive oil for 4 minutes to get them soft.

2. Add water, tomato juice, and barley. Stir.

3. Add chili powder, parsley, and bay leaves. Stir.

4. Cover and cook for 20 minutes. Add veggie burgers and cook for another 5 minutes.

5. Season with salt and pepper, and remember to remove the bay leaves before eating.

# Barley Pilaf with Edamame and Roasted Red Pepper

Serves 6

This atypical pilaf recipe brings in a ton of unexpected flavors, plus added protein from the edamame. This dish tastes great both warm and cold. Thus, it's adaptable if you need a Dish of Revenge to throw at an unsuspecting someone. (Revenge *is* a dish best served cold, after all.) See, this isn't just a cookbook. It's a Life book.

2 cups frozen shelled edamame, thawed and drained

2 cups cooked barley

½ cup roasted red peppers

⅔ cup green peas

⅔ cup corn, fresh or thawed frozen

1½ tablespoons Dijon mustard

2 tablespoons lemon juice

¾ teaspoon garlic powder

2 tablespoons olive oil

Salt and pepper to taste

½ cup chopped fresh cilantro

1 avocado, diced

1. Mix edamame, barley, peppers, peas, and corn in a bowl. Give them a good toss.

2. In another bowl, whisk together mustard, lemon juice, garlic powder, and olive oil. Pour over barley mixture. Season with salt, pepper, and cilantro. Toss and then top with avocado.

# Quinoa "Tapioca" Pudding

Serves 4

An untraditional dessert pudding, using healthy quinoa rather than rice. Delicious and creamy, this dish pairs nicely with a hot vegan cappuccino.

1 cup quinoa

2 cups water

2 cups soy cream

2 tablespoons maple syrup

1 teaspoon cornstarch

2 bananas, sliced

½ teaspoon almond extract

⅓ cup raisins

Dash nutmeg

1. In a stock pot over high heat, add quinoa and water. Reduce heat to low and simmer, covered, for 15 minutes. It will be done when all the water is absorbed.

2. Add soy cream, maple syrup, cornstarch, and bananas. Stir frequently, cooking for another 8 minutes on low heat.

3. Remove from heat. Stir in almond extract and raisins and sprinkle with a dash of nutmeg.

# Spiced Couscous Salad with Bell Pepper and Zucchini

## Serves 4

Couscous resembles the size and texture of pastina pasta, but is whole grain semolina. This dish is a combination of Middle Eastern spices and vegetables. A perfect side dish or meal itself. Just toast some whole grain pita bread and crunch away.

2 cups vegetable broth

2 cups couscous

1 teaspoon cumin

½ teaspoon turmeric

½ teaspoon paprika

¼ teaspoon cayenne pepper

1 tablespoon lemon juice

2 zucchini, sliced

1 red bell pepper, chopped

1 yellow bell pepper, chopped

3 cloves garlic, minced

½ white onion, chopped

2 tablespoons olive oil

2 tablespoons chopped fresh parsley

Salt and pepper

1. In a large stock pot over medium heat, mix vegetable broth and couscous, bringing broth to a boil. Add cumin, turmeric, paprika, and cayenne pepper and stir.

2. Shut the heat off and cover the pot, leaving the couscous to sit for 15 minutes. The liquid should be fully absorbed when the time is up. Add lemon juice and mix, mix, mix.

3. In a medium saucepan over medium-high heat, sauté the peppers, garlic, and onion in the olive oil, about 5 minutes. Mix into the couscous. Add the parsley and salt and pepper. Give yourself a pat on the back.

# Orange and Raisin Curried Couscous

Serves 4

Lots of whole grains taste fabulous when morphed from savory to sweet. This pilaf brings the bright sweet notes of orange and combines them with the punch of coriander and curry. A spicy-sweet mix perfect served warm. Try baking up a raisin bread version of traditional naan to enhance the warm flavors.

2 cups water

1½ cups couscous

½ cup orange juice

1 onion, chopped

2 tablespoons extra virgin olive oil

½ teaspoon coriander powder

½ teaspoon curry powder

3 dates, chopped

¾ cup golden raisins

¾ cup sliced almonds

2 scallions, chopped

1. In a large saucepan, bring water to a boil and add couscous. Remove from heat, stir in orange juice, cover, and allow to sit for 15 minutes.

2. In a small skillet over medium-high heat, sauté onion in olive oil for about 2 minutes. Add coriander powder, curry powder, and chopped dates. Cook for another 1 minute. Take off heat and add mixture to couscous, mixing well.

3. Top with raisins, almonds, and scallions. Serve!

# Tropical Couscous

Serves 2

Sweet—and full of island flavor. The chopped almonds give a satisfying crunch, and the sliced fresh melon makes a cool addition to the dish. If you're really in a Caribbean mindset, drink with a fresh papaya smoothie. And if you get the urge to begin a hula dance while taking your first bite, by all means, go for it.

1 cup coconut milk

1 cup pineapple juice (or orange juice)

1 cup couscous

½ teaspoon vanilla

2 tablespoons agave nectar (light)

¼ cup chopped almonds

½ cup sliced honeydew melon

1. In a medium saucepan over low heat, bring the coconut milk and pineapple juice to a simmer. Don't boil this one.

2. Add the couscous and let cook for 1 minute. Add vanilla. Shut the heat off, letting everything sit for 5 minutes.

3. Stir in agave, almonds, and melon.

**THE** SKINNY **ON . . . Agave nectar**

Agave nectar comes in two varieties: "light" or "amber." Like maple syrup grades A or B, agave flavor varies from intense to more mild. Amber agave has a stronger flavor, whereas light agave simply tastes more like generic sugar.

# Confetti "Rice"

**Serves 6**

Use in corn tortillas instead of taco meat, or on top of a salad for a Mexican twist. Any recipe with the word *confetti* in it has to be delicious and fun. Just don't throw it in the air or anything. Or, at least taste it first. *Then* you can throw it in the air.

1 onion, chopped

2 cloves garlic, minced

2 tablespoons olive oil

1 cup barley

1 (15-ounce) can diced tomatoes

1 tablespoon soy sauce

2 cups vegetable broth

1 teaspoon cumin

1 teaspoon chili powder

½ teaspoon cayenne pepper

1 teaspoon onion powder

1 cup frozen corn

1 teaspoon parsley

½ teaspoon salt

1. In a stock pot over medium-high heat, sauté onion and garlic in olive oil. Add the barley and stir, allowing to brown. Toast for 1 minute.

2. Add the canned tomatoes (plus the juice in the can), soy sauce, and veggie broth. Stir well and add cumin, chili powder, cayenne pepper, and onion powder. Cook for 15 minutes.

3. Add frozen corn, parsley, and salt. Cook for another 5 minutes and serve.

# Barley and Bell Pepper Chili

Serves 6

Hearty and satisfying thanks to crunchy whole grains used in place of beef. The bell pepper and dash of nutmeg give a sweet tinge to the traditionally spicy chili dish. Sweet and spicy? My dream date. Yes, I'm talking about my dream date being a dinner plate again. So sue me.

3 cloves garlic, minced

1 onion, chopped

2 red bell peppers, chopped

2 tablespoons olive oil

½ cup barley

2½ cups veggie broth

1 (15-ounce) can diced tomatoes

1 (15-ounce) can black beans

2 tablespoons chili powder

1 teaspoon cumin

½ teaspoon oregano

½ teaspoon nutmeg

2 tablespoons chopped fresh cilantro

1. In a large stew pot over medium-high heat, sauté garlic, onion, and peppers in the olive oil for 3 minutes. Add the barley and toast for 1 minute. It should become brownish. FYI, toasting things is so fun!

2. Reduce heat to low and add the veggie broth, tomatoes, beans, chili powder, cumin, oregano, and nutmeg. Let simmer, cover, and cook for 35 minutes. Top with cilantro before serving.

# Fruity Fall Quinoa

**Serves 4**

If you want to keep this sweet, simply omit the parsley, thyme, celery, and onion. That way you can eat it warm for breakfast on a cool day. You can sweeten quinoa dishes even more by subbing almond or soy milk for water.

1 cup red or white quinoa

2 cups apple juice

1 cup water

½ onion, diced

2 ribs celery, diced

2 tablespoons vegan margarine

½ teaspoon nutmeg

½ teaspoon cinnamon

¼ teaspoon cloves

½ cup dried cranberries

½ cup dried apricots, chopped

1 teaspoon thyme

1 teaspoon parsley

¼ teaspoon salt

1. In a large stock pot, combine quinoa with apple juice and water. Bring to a boil then let simmer for 15 minutes.

2. In medium saucepan over medium-high heat, melt margarine and sauté onion and celery for about 4 minutes or until soft. Add to the quinoa mixture and stir for 1 minute.

3. Toss in all other ingredients and cook over the stove on low heat for 4 minutes. Just warm it up and let all the flavors mingle. You know: meet, greet, have a good time.

## PART-TIME TIP

Stir-frying is quite possibly the easiest and quickest way to whip up a meal. Since stir-frying requires you to cook at high temps, try to keep an arm's length away from your wok to avoid painful oil burns. I learned this the hard way in the days of yore.

# Couscous and Bean Pilaf

Serves 4

We've been tossing beans, pilafs, and couscous around here for a while. We might as well combine them! The real invention in cooking comes when you have only certain ingredients left in the house. You ask yourself, what the *hell* am I going to make? And then *voila*, your masterpiece somehow comes to life using veggie broth, beans, and parsley.

2 cups vegetable broth

2 cups couscous

2 tablespoons olive oil

2 tablespoons red wine vinegar

½ teaspoon crushed red pepper flakes

2 tablespoons minced pimento peppers

1 tablespoon chopped fresh parsley

1 (15-ounce) can cannellini beans

Salt and pepper to taste

1. In a large stock pot over medium-low heat, bring veggie broth to a simmer. Then drop couscous in. Cover and let cook for 15 minutes.

2. In a small bowl, mix the olive oil and red wine vinegar. It's best if you use a whisk to do this, I find. Add the red pepper flakes. Pour over couscous.

3. Fluff in the pimento peppers, parsley, and beans. Season with salt and pepper.

# Barley Baked Beans

Serves 8

Rich but not heavy, this dish has the sweet molasses flavor of traditional baked beans. This is a side that would go perfectly with roasted corn and vegan ribs. (Yep, many varieties of vegan barbeque are available in the frozen foods section of your grocery store.) Kick back with a cold beer and try this dish at your next barbecue.

2 cups cooked barley

2 (15-ounce) cans pinto beans

1 onion, diced

1 (28-ounce) can crushed tomatoes

½ cup water

¼ cup brown sugar

⅓ cup vegan barbeque sauce

2 tablespoons molasses

2 teaspoons mustard powder

1 teaspoon garlic powder

1 teaspoon salt

1. Preheat oven to 300°F.

2. Combine all ingredients in a large casserole dish, cover, and bake for 2 hours.

3. Uncover and cook for another 15 minutes. Finger lickin' good, chief.

# CHAPTER 11

# Tofu

## *BELIEVE IT OR NOT, CAN ACTUALLY TASTE GOOD*

The other, other white meat. Tofu is a lean, mean protein machine. Low in calories and low in fat, it will fill you up to bursting and still keep your stomach from commanding a siege over the edge of your pants when you sit down. (I know you know what I mean.)

# Cajun-Spiced Cornmeal-Breaded Tofu

Serves 3

A recipe that brings to mind breaded catfish. There is not a way in the world I can say no to a spicy Cajun recipe. Those two words should be synonymous with delicious. Cajun deliciousness may cause fits of joy. And that's no voodoo.

⅔ cup soy milk

2 tablespoons lime juice

¼ cup flour (white or whole wheat)

⅓ cup cornmeal

1 tablespoon Cajun seasoning

1 teaspoon onion powder

½ teaspoon salt

½ teaspoon black pepper

½ teaspoon cayenne pepper

1 pound block firm tofu, well-pressed

Canola oil for frying

1. Preheat oven to 350°F. With vegan margarine grease your baking dish. (Or you will be very sad come eatin' time.)

2. In a large, shallow bowl (or any bowl—what is this, math class?), combine the soy milk and lime juice. Whisk well.

3. In another bowl, mix up the flour, cornmeal, Cajun seasoning, onion powder, salt, pepper, and cayenne pepper.

4. Cut the tofu into manageable strips. One at a time, dip them in the soy mixture and then coat them with the flour mixture.

5. Add strips of tofu to the baking dish and cook in the oven for 10 minutes. Or you could always pan-fry your tofu strips in a tablespoon of canola oil for a good 3 minutes on each side. Serve with hot sauce or barbeque sauce and warm pilaf.

# Mexican-Spice Crusted Tofu with Cashew Sour Cream

Serves 3

Don't bother checking your calendar, *amigos*. It's not Cinco de Mayo, but that doesn't mean we can't celebrate this amazing dish that you—yes you—can make. This is a great rice topper or substitute to use for taco "meat" in corn or lettuce taco shells. Add some black beans and you've got yourself a satisfying meal.

2 tablespoons soy sauce

3 tablespoons hot chili sauce

1 teaspoon sugar

1 pound block extra-firm tofu, sliced into strips

1 teaspoon garlic powder

1 teaspoon onion powder

1 tablespoon chili powder

¾ teaspoon cumin

¾ teaspoon oregano

2 tablespoons flour

1. Preheat oven to 350°F.

2. In a bowl large enough for dipping, whisk the soy sauce, chili sauce, and sugar. Add the tofu and let marinate for 1½ hours.

3. Mix remaining ingredients in a separate dish. Carefully rub tofu into spice mix on both sides, and place on a lightly greased baking sheet. Bake for 9 minutes, turning once.

**To Make the Cashew Sour Cream Dipping Sauce**

½ cup raw cashews soaked for an hour or more

½ cup water

1½ tablespoons lemon juice

3–4 teaspoons apple cider vinegar

1. Food process the cashews, water, lemon juice, and apple cider vinegar. Spoon into bowl for a dipping sauce.

# Pineapple-Glazed Tofu

Serves 3

A great dish for hot weather days. Serve with a little rice and a light green salad. You'll soon be cool as a cucumber. I mean, pineapple.

½ cup pineapple preserves

2 tablespoons balsamic vinegar

2 tablespoons soy sauce

⅔ cup pineapple juice

1 pound block extra-firm tofu, cubed

2 tablespoons flour

2 tablespoons coconut oil

1 tablespoon cornstarch

1.  Whisk the pineapple preserves, balsamic vinegar, soy sauce, and pineapple juice together.

2.  Coat the tofu with flour.

3.  In a medium saucepan over medium heat, sauté the tofu in oil until golden. Take the heat down to medium-low and add the pineapple sauce mixture to the tofu. Stir.

4.  Cook for 4 minutes before adding the cornstarch in. Whisk to avoid lumps. Allow sauce to thicken up for a few minutes and aloha, you're done.

# Tofu "Fish" Sticks

### Serves 3

The seaweed in this recipe lends a "fish"-like taste for all you undersea aficionados. Please, do have a whale of a time with this recipe—I won't water it down for you; it's fabulous!

½ cup flour

½ cup soy milk

2 tablespoons lemon juice

2 tablespoons dulse seaweed flakes or kelp

1 tablespoon Old Bay seasoning blend

1 teaspoon onion powder

1½ cup fine ground bread crumbs

1 pound block extra-firm tofu, well pressed

1.  Preheat oven to 350°F.

2.  Set up three bowls. Fill one with the flour. Add the soy milk and lemon juice to the second. In the third, mix together the seaweed flakes or kelp, Old Bay seasoning, onion powder, and bread crumbs.

3.  Slice tofu into 12 strips, about ½" each. Coat each strip with flour, dip it into soy milk mix, and then dip it into the bread crumb mix. Coat them well—it gets cold underwater!

4.  Place on a cookie sheet lightly greased with vegan margarine and bake for 20 minutes, turning over once, and baking for another 10 minutes. Serve with ketchup!

# Indian Tofu Palak

Serves 4

A typical palak paneer is a dish of cheese and creamed spinach. Of course, we use tofu—the Magical White Block of Wonder—to meet all of our vegan needs.

3 cloves garlic, minced

1 pound block extra-firm tofu, chopped into cubes

2 tablespoons olive oil

2 tablespoons nutritional yeast

½ teaspoon onion powder

4 bunches fresh spinach

3 tablespoons water

1 tablespoon curry powder

2 teaspoons cumin

½ teaspoon salt

½ cup plain soy yogurt

1. In a medium saucepan on low heat, sauté the garlic and tofu for 1 minute in the olive oil. Add the nutritional yeast and onion powder, stirring to coat tofu. Cook for 3 minutes until tofu is browned.

2. Add the spinach, water, curry powder, cumin, and salt. As the spinach wilts (sad spinach), add the soy yogurt and heat until the spinach is soft. This will only take about 1 minutes. Enjoy!

# Tofu "Chicken" Nuggets

**Serves 4**

Who can possibly resist the temptation of chicken nuggets? Even if you are vegan or vegetarian, you may still long for the unforgettable and highly processed (but still scrumptious) flavor of the chicken nuggets in kids' meals everywhere. Now fast forward: Here's stellar, sophisticated, adult, intelligent you. Still a kid at heart, now you can revisit the culinary delights of childhood with nary a concern.

2 tablespoons mustard

¼ cup soy milk

3 tablespoons nutritional yeast

½ cup bread crumbs

½ cup flour

1 teaspoon garlic powder

1 teaspoon onion powder

½ teaspoon salt

¼ teaspoon pepper

1 teaspoon poultry seasoning

1 pound block extra-firm tofu, sliced into strips

1. Preheat oven to 350°F.

2. In a small bowl, whisk together the mustard, soy milk, and nutritional yeast.

3. In another bowl, mix the bread crumbs, flour, garlic powder, onion powder, salt, pepper, and poultry seasoning.

4. Coat the strips of tofu in the soy milk mix, and then dip them in the bread crumb mix. Cover them well so they get nice and crunchy once cooked!

5. Bake in the oven on a cookie sheet lightly greased with vegan margarine for 20 minutes, carefully turning over once. Serve with ketchup or sweet and sour sauce!

# Lemon Basil Tofu

**Serves 6**

Tart and zesty. This chewy tofu dish tastes great over angel hair pasta with a little vegan margarine and nutritional yeast. And throw some wine in there, too. (You deserve it; it's the middle of the week, after all.)

3 tablespoons lemon juice

1 tablespoon soy sauce

2 teaspoons apple cider vinegar

1 tablespoon Dijon mustard

¾ teaspoon sugar

3 tablespoons olive oil

2 tablespoons chopped fresh basil

2 (1 pound) blocks extra-firm tofu, pressed

1. Whisk all ingredients except the tofu in a small bowl, and pour into a wide casserole dish.

2. Slice up the tofu in ½"-thick pieces.

3. Place tofu in marinade, cover tightly, and let sit in the fridge for 2–3 hours.

4. Preheat oven to 350°F.

5. Cook for 15 minutes on a baking sheet greased with vegan margarine, and then turn them over. Cook for another 12 minutes and eat! You can use the remaining marinade over pasta as well.

# Tofu BBQ Sauce "Steaks"

**Serves 4**

Tofu "steaks" are perfect for a mock roast beef sandwich. Perhaps you are just in the mood to be a Real Man and eat some meat. I understand. I get that urge all the time. So go ahead, be a Real Man*. You could fool Davy Crockett with flavor like this!
*(Admittedly, Tofu Steak may be slightly less Manly.)

¼ cup vegan barbecue sauce

¼ cup water

2 teaspoons balsamic vinegar

2 tablespoons soy sauce

1–2 tablespoons hot sauce

2 teaspoons sugar

2 (1 pound) blocks extra-firm tofu, pressed

½ onion, chopped

2 tablespoons olive oil

1. Whisk barbecue sauce, water, vinegar, soy sauce, hot sauce, and sugar in a small bowl. Set aside.

2. Slice tofu into ½"-thick strips.

3. In a large saucepan over medium-high heat, sauté the onion in the olive oil. Add the tofu. Fry until golden, about 2 minutes on each side.

4. Lower the heat to medium and add the sauce mixture. Coat tofu and stir for about 6 minutes, until the sauce thickens up. Pull on your (faux) coonskin cap and load the (toy dart) rifle! Eat!

# Braised Tofu and Veggie Cacciatore

Serves 4

Delicious over pasta, but my mother always put cacciatore over rice. Brown rice would be a perfect complement along with the nice glass (or two . . . three . . .) of red wine.

½ yellow onion, chopped

½ cup mushrooms, sliced

1 carrot, chopped

3 cloves garlic, minced

2 (1 pound) blocks extra-firm tofu, chopped into cubes

2 tablespoons olive oil

½ cup white cooking wine

3 large fresh tomatoes, diced

1 (6-ounce) can tomato paste

1 bay leaf

½ teaspoon salt

1 teaspoon dried parsley

1 teaspoon oregano

1 teaspoon basil

1. In a large saucepan over medium-high heat, sauté onion, mushrooms, carrot, garlic, and tofu in olive oil for 5 minutes.

2. Reduce heat to medium-low and add the cooking wine, diced tomatoes, tomato paste, bay leaf, salt, and other spices. Stir up well. It'll smell heavenly.

3. Cover the pan and let simmer for 20 minutes. Stir every once in a while and don't forget to take out that pesky bay leaf before eating.

# Tofu "Ricotta" Manicotti

**Serves 4**

In vegan cooking, one of our very best friends is the quotation mark. We like to say "Ricotta" or "Steak" or "Beef." Basically, we own anything that can be encapsulated by two quotation marks. Quotations marks should then in our case be synonymous for the word awesome. Please enjoy this veganized Tofu Awesome Ricotta Awesome Manicotti.

12 large manicotti

2 (1 pound) blocks firm tofu, crumbled

2 tablespoons lemon juice

2 tablespoons olive oil

2 tablespoons soy milk

¼ cup nutritional yeast

½ teaspoon garlic powder

½ teaspoon onion powder

½ teaspoon salt

1 teaspoon basil

2 tablespoons fresh chopped parsley

2 cups prepared marinara sauce

⅓ cup grated vegan cheese (optional)

1. Preheat the oven to 350°F. Cook manicotti according to the instructions on the package.

2. Mash up the tofu, lemon juice, olive oil, soy milk, nutritional yeast, garlic powder, onion powder, salt, basil, and parsley in a large bowl. Mix well until the consistency is almost smooth.

3. Stuff the manicotti with the tofu! Don't let them burst, though. You don't want their little intestines to explode all over the place. (Sorry, that was gross.)

4. Cover the bottom of a casserole dish with the marinara sauce and line up the manicotti inside. Cover with vegan shredded cheese and remaining sauce. Bake for 30 minutes.

# Easy Fried Tofu

Serves 3

In this case, it's all in the name, folks. An easy, tasty dish that you can munch on as a snack when the 3:00 P.M. hunger monster creeps up on you. With this, you shall defeat him valiantly.

1 pound block extra-firm tofu, cubed

¼ cup soy sauce (optional)

2 tablespoons flour

2 tablespoons nutritional yeast

1 teaspoon garlic powder

¼ teaspoon salt

Dash pepper

Canola oil for frying

1. If you're up to it, marinade the tofu in the soy sauce for an hour. Skip this step if you want and cut out the soy sauce altogether.

2. Mix the flour, nutritional yeast, garlic powder, salt, and pepper in a bowl.

3. Coat the pieces of tofu in the flour mixture.

4. In a medium skillet over medium heat, heat the oil and fry the tofu for 5 minutes on both sides. Just cook until golden. (And you thought fried food was bad for you.)

# Saucy Kung Pao Tofu

Serves 6

This dish packs a wallop and a POW! (If this dish were a comic book page, you would have just been knocked out by big yellow type!) Cook tofu with some bamboo shoots or Asian noodles, or some snap peas and carrots.

3 tablespoons soy sauce

2 tablespoons rice vinegar

1 tablespoon sesame oil

2 (1 pound) blocks firm tofu, chopped

1 red bell pepper, chopped

⅔ cup sliced mushrooms

3 cloves garlic

2 small red or green chili peppers, diced

1 teaspoon red pepper flakes

2 tablespoons oil

1 teaspoon ground ginger

½ cup vegetable broth

½ teaspoon sugar

1½ teaspoons cornstarch

2 green onions, chopped

½ cup peanuts

1. In a small bowl, whisk together the soy sauce, rice vinegar, and sesame oil. Pour into a shallow dish. Add the tofu and let it marinate for 1 hour. Drain and save the marinade sauce when finished.

2. In a large saucepan over medium-high heat, sauté the bell peppers, mushrooms, garlic, chilies, and red pepper flakes in the oil for 3 minutes. Add the tofu and cook for another 2 minutes until the vegetables have become soft and brightly colored.

3. Lower the heat to medium and add the reserved marinade, ginger powder, veggie broth, sugar, and cornstarch. You have to make certain to whisk this so the cornstarch doesn't become lumpy and strange looking. Stir consistently and let the sauce thicken up.

4. Lastly, add the green onions and peanuts, heating for a final 1 minute. POW!

# Sticky Teriyaki Tofu Cubes

Serves 3

What do you *do* with Sticky Teriyaki Tofu Cubes? First, be prepared to be blown away by how great these taste. Next, toss them in a salad, or eat them as a snack in the office. But the world is your vegan oyster. Do as your heart desires.

⅓ cup soy sauce

3 tablespoons barbecue sauce

2 teaspoons hot chili sauce

¼ cup maple syrup

¾ teaspoon garlic powder

1 pound block extra-firm tofu, cut into thin chunks

1. Preheat the oven to 375°F.

2. In a casserole dish, whisk all ingredients except the tofu.

3. Add the tofu and stir to make sure it is well-covered.

4. Bake for 40 minutes, tossing once.

# Simmered Coconut Curried Tofu

**Serves 3**

This dish can be served atop any tropical-flavored rice, or even as a toothpick appetizer alongside mango salsa and chips.

1 pound block extra-firm tofu, cubed

1 tablespoon olive oil

2 teaspoons sesame oil

3 tablespoons peanut butter

2 tablespoons soy sauce

2 tablespoons water

1 teaspoon curry powder

¼ cup coconut flakes

2 tablespoons fresh cilantro, minced

1. In a large saucepan over medium-high heat, sauté the tofu in the olive oil until it turns slightly golden.

2. Lower the heat to medium-low. Add the sesame oil, peanut butter, soy sauce, water, and curry powder. Stir well and heat for about 5 minutes.

3. Add the coconut flakes and cilantro and heat for another 1 minute. Don't leave on any longer. Eat up!

# Agave Mustard Glazed Tofu

Serves 3

A sweet and zesty dish perfect with some Vegan Baked Beans (see Chapters 10 and 12 for recipes), or at a barbecue with vegan dogs and veggie burgers. And, you know, beer.

2 tablespoons lemon juice

2 tablespoons water

1 teaspoon soy sauce

¼ cup agave nectar

2 tablespoons prepared mustard

½ teaspoon garlic powder

½ teaspoon sugar

¾ teaspoon curry powder (optional)

1 pound block extra-firm tofu, chopped into cubes

1. In a small bowl, whisk up all the ingredients except the tofu. Place the tofu in a casserole dish and add the marinade. Let marinate for 1 hour, stirring occasionally so that all portions of the tofu are evenly covered. They have to learn to share!

2. Preheat the oven to 400°F.

3. Put the casserole dish in the oven and bake for 25 minutes.

# Mexico City Protein Bowl

**Serves 1**

A meal for *uno*. Yes, that's it. You and only you, my dear.

½ pound block tofu, diced small

1 scallion, chopped

1 tablespoon olive oil

½ cup peas

½ cup corn

½ teaspoon chili powder

1 can black beans, drained

2 corn tortillas

Hot sauce, to taste

1. In a large saucepan over medium heat, cook the tofu and the scallions in the olive oil for 3 minutes. Then add the peas, corn, and chili powder. Stir frequently while you continue cooking for another 2 minutes.

2. Lower the heat to medium-low, and add the black beans. Cook for 5 minutes.

3. Spoon the mixture onto the corn tortillas. (Rest them at the bottom of a bowl for this to be a "Protein Bowl.") Season with hot sauce!

## PART-TIME TIP

This recipe has a walloping 66 grams of protein. But beware! There are also 1,198 calories per serving. While not a lot if you eat wisely throughout the rest of the day, make certain to take care. Split up the dish for lunch and a side of dinner if that helps. No one likes overeating. It sucks.

# Orange Glazed "Chicken" Tofu

Serves 3

In the style of your favorite Chinese take-out restaurant, I present to you Orange "Chicken." Eat it with a side of rice and steamed veggies to complete that lazy evening feel.

2 tablespoons soy sauce

⅔ cup orange juice

2 tablespoons rice vinegar

1 tablespoon maple syrup

½ teaspoon red pepper flakes

1 pound block firm tofu, well pressed and chopped

3 cloves garlic, minced

2 tablespoons olive oil

1½ teaspoons cornstarch

2 tablespoons water

1. In a small bowl, whisk up the soy sauce, OJ, vinegar, syrup, and red pepper flakes.

2. In a medium saucepan over medium heat, sauté the tofu and garlic in the olive oil for 2 minutes until lightly brown.

3. Lower the heat to medium-low and add the OJ mixture. Bring to a simmer slowly and cook for 8 more minutes.

4. Whisk up the cornstarch and water in another small bowl. Keep stirring until the starch is dissolved—sometimes it can be pesky. Add this mixture to the tofu mixture.

5. Allow to come to a simmer once more and cook for 4 minutes.

# Chili and Curry Baked Tofu

Serves 3

For those with a romantic attachment to spice, a delivery from Yours Truly. Enjoy the Indian-Thai fusion flavors of this dish. Serve with rice, or some lentils and vegan naan.

⅓ cup coconut milk

2 tablespoons maple syrup

3 small chilies, minced

½ teaspoon garlic powder

1 teaspoon cumin

1 teaspoon curry

½ teaspoon turmeric

1 pound block extra-firm tofu, sliced thin

1. In a small bowl, whisk up the coconut milk, maple syrup, chilies, garlic powder, cumin, curry, and turmeric. Pour in a shallow dish. Toss in the tofu and let marinate for 1 hour.

2. Preheat the oven to 425°F.

3. Move the tofu into a casserole dish. Pour 3 teaspoons of the marinade over the tofu, and reserve the rest for after the tofu is cooked. Bake for 10 minutes, then turn over and bake for another 10. The reserved marinade can be used as dipping sauce.

# Beer-Battered Tofu Fillet

Serves 8

Who needs eggs when beer is sticky enough to hold any batter? No one, that's who.

2 teaspoons garlic powder

2 teaspoons onion powder

2 teaspoons paprika

1 teaspoon salt

½ teaspoon black pepper

3 (1 pound) blocks extra-firm tofu, chopped chunky

1 (12-ounce) bottle of beer

1½ cups whole wheat flour

Canola oil for sautéing

1. In a small bowl, mix the garlic powder, onion powder, paprika, salt, and pepper. Pat the pieces of tofu into the mixture. Pat lightly but make sure it sticks.

2. Pour the beer into a large bowl and add the flour. Stir well. Dip the tofu into the beer batter.

3. In a medium sized skillet over medium heat, heat the oil and sauté the tofu until crispy and crunchy on all sides.

# Spicy Chili-Basil Tofu

Serves 3

A popular dish in Thailand that is most frequently made with fish. Obviously there's nothing fishy about this recipe—only tofushy.

4 cloves garlic, minced

5 small red or green chilies, diced

3 shallots, diced

2 tablespoons sesame oil

1 pound block firm tofu, diced

1 teaspoon sugar

¼ cup soy sauce

1 tablespoon vegetarian oyster sauce

1 bunch Thai basil leaves, whole (you can use regular basil, but the taste won't be as pronounced)

1. In a large saucepan over medium heat, add the garlic, chilies, and shallots and cook in the oil for 4 minutes. Allow them to brown.

2. Add the tofu and cook for 3 minutes. Allow the tofu to brown as well.

3. Lower the heat to medium-low. Add the oyster sauce, sugar, and soy sauce. Mix well to dissolve the sugar. Cook for another 4 minutes and stir in the basil leaves, allowing them to wilt. Enjoy with some rice!

# CHAPTER 12

# Seitan, TVP, and Tempeh

## *NEW BFFLS**

Some new friends to mingle with your old friends. I promise they're not intimidating. (Otherwise, I'd have been too afraid to talk to them in the first place.) (*Best Friends For Life)

## Pineapple TVP Baked Beans

PROTEIN
FIBER
FLEX
QUICK

Serves 4

Add a splash of the tropics to the sweet and tangy flavor of traditional baked beans. The TVP adds protein to keep you fuller longer, and the pineapple enhances the sweetness of the barbecue sauce without being overpowering.

2 (15-ounce) cans black beans, partially drained

1 onion, diced

⅔ cup barbecue sauce

2 tablespoons prepared mustard

2 tablespoons brown sugar

1 cup TVP

1 cup hot water

1 (8-ounce) can diced pineapple, drained

¼ teaspoon salt

½ teaspoon pepper

1. In a large saucepan on low heat, simmer the beans, onion, barbecue sauce, mustard, and brown sugar. Cover and cook for 10 minutes.

2. Mix the TVP with the hot water and let it sit for 6 minutes to rehydrate. Drain well.

3. Add the TVP, pineapple, salt, and pepper to the bean mixture and simmer for another 12 minutes. Then, thanks to the TVP you'll be saying TTYL to hunger!

## Spicy Seitan Taco "Meat"

PROTEIN
FLEX
QUICK

Serves 6

You can also make taco "meat" out of black beans or TVP. But seitan taco "meat" is better if you're looking for strip-shaped meat.

½ onion, diced

½ green bell pepper, chopped small

1 large tomato, chopped

1 (16-ounce) package prepared seitan, chopped (about 2½ cups)

2 tablespoons olive oil

1 tablespoon soy sauce

1 teaspoon hot sauce

2 tablespoons chili powder

½ teaspoon cumin

6 soft taco shells

1. In a large saucepan over medium-high heat, sauté the onion, pepper, tomato, and seitan in the olive oil. Make sure you brown the seitan.

2. Add in the soy sauce, hot sauce, chili powder, and cumin. Cook for 1 minute and serve in soft taco shells!

# Rosemary Tempeh Hash

Serves 4

Less greasy than a normal hash, and packed with tempeh protein. Tempeh has a natural nutty flavor that lends itself well to the earthy flavor of the potatoes and rosemary. Yay, nature.

2 potatoes, boiled and diced

1 (8-ounce) package tempeh, diced

2 tablespoons olive oil

2 green onions, chopped

1 tablespoon chili powder

1 teaspoon rosemary

Salt and pepper to taste

1. In a large saucepan over medium heat, sauté the cooked potatoes and the diced tempeh in the olive oil for 3 minutes.

2. Add all other ingredients to the pan. Stir and cook for another 4 minutes. *Voila.*

# Basic Baked Tempeh Patties

Serves 4

Tempeh patties make great veggie burgers! There are tons of varieties of tempeh available, from seven grain to spicy, and even bacon-flavored. I like to think of tempeh as an adventure because it originally came all the way from Indonesia.

1 (8-ounce) package tempeh

1 cup vegetable broth plus 2 tablespoons

3 tablespoons soy sauce

2 tablespoons apple cider vinegar

3 cloves garlic, minced

2 teaspoons sesame oil

1. Cut up tempeh into desired shape. The recipe works best if patties are shaped close to "quarter pounder" size. In a medium saucepan over medium-low heat simmer in 1 cup veggie broth for 10 minutes. Drain when finished.

2. Whisk up all the other ingredients, including the 2 tablespoons of veggie broth. Marinate the tempeh for a few hours. Preheat the oven to 375°F.

3. Cook tempeh on a greased baking sheet for 12 minutes on each side. *Finit*! Serve on whole wheat rolls with lettuce and tomato. Mm, mm.

# Southern-Fried Seitan

Serves 4

Veganism can be healthy. But it can also be decadent. Deep-fried seitan is as good as any chicken-fried steak comes. I would tempt you and say fry up an "accidentally vegan" candy bar for dessert . . . but I'm too nice for that.

2 tablespoons soy sauce

¼ cup soy milk

2 tablespoons mustard

⅔ cup flour

¼ cup nutritional yeast

1 tablespoon baking powder

1 teaspoon garlic powder

1 teaspoon onion powder

½ teaspoon paprika

½ teaspoon salt

½ teaspoon black pepper

1 (16-ounce) package prepared seitan

Canola oil for frying

1. In a small bowl, mix the soy sauce, soy milk, and mustard.

2. In another bowl, mix the remaining ingredients except for the seitan and frying oil.

3. Coat the seitan pieces first in the milk mixture, and then in the flour mixture.

4. In a medium saucepan over medium heat, heat the oil. Fry the seitan until golden brown in the oil, about 4 minutes altogether. Drain on paper towels.

# Basic Homemade Seitan

**Serves 8**

Homemade seitan is less expensive than store-bought. It takes a while to cook, so it's sort of a pain if you're pressed for time, but it's a good option if you're interested in creating your own from scratch and saving it for later use. After all, as Mom says, homemade is always better than store-bought.

1 cup vital wheat gluten

1 teaspoon onion powder

1 teaspoon garlic powder

6 cups plus ¾ cup strong vegetable broth

2 tablespoons soy sauce

### THE SKINNY ON ... Vital Wheat Gluten

Vital wheat gluten is used in recipes to improve the stretchy quality of dough. It is the natural protein found in wheat flour, and is always used in seitan cooking. With 75 percent protein, it packs a powerful nutritional punch into any recipe. Many natural foods stores carry vital wheat gluten, but it's also readily available online.

1.  In a medium bowl, mix together the wheat gluten, onion powder, and garlic powder. In a different small bowl, mix the ¾ cup veggie broth with the soy sauce.

2.  Slowly add the broth mixture to the wheat gluten mixture, kneading with your hands until the wheat gluten forms a ball of dough.

3.  Continue kneading the dough until the texture is universally smooth. Allow to sit for a few minutes, and knead again for 3 minutes.

4.  Divide the dough into 4 pieces, ½" thick.

5.  In a large stock pot over medium heat, bring 6 cups of vegetable broth to a simmer. Add the dough pieces and continue to simmer for 1 hour on low heat. Drain the broth, save for later in the fridge, or add to your favorite seitan dish. Seitan can be stored in the fridge for up to a week, and in the freezer it's good for a month.

# Massaman Curried Seitan

Serves 4

A popular dish in Muslim countries, Thailand, and India. It's nice to try something a little different now and then. Unless, of course, you are Muslim, Thai, or Indian. In which case, by all means . . . carry on.

1 tablespoon Chinese five-spice seasoning

½ teaspoon fresh ginger, grated

½ teaspoon turmeric

¼ teaspoon cayenne pepper to taste

1 tablespoon sesame oil

1 cup vegetable broth

1½ cups coconut milk

2 potatoes, chopped

1½ cups seitan, chopped small

2 whole cloves

1 teaspoon salt

1 tablespoon peanut butter

½ teaspoon cinnamon

2 teaspoons brown sugar

⅓ cup cashews

1. In a stock pot over medium heat, combine the five-spice seasoning, ginger, turmeric, and cayenne in the sesame oil. Stir continuously for 1 minute.

2. Reduce heat to medium-low and add the veggie broth and the coconut milk. Then add the potatoes, seitan, cloves, and salt. Cover and cook for 20 minutes. Come back every so often and give it another stir.

3. When 20 minutes have passed, uncover. Add the peanut butter, cinnamon, sugar, and cashews. Cook for 1 minute longer and serve warm!

# Homemade Baked BBQ Seitan

**Serves 8**

In this recipe you bake, rather than boil, the homemade seitan. This version works well for sandwiches and is warm right out of the oven. I prefer to bake seitan, personally. This recipe yields a lunch "meat"-style seitan, that can be sliced and put into sandwiches!

1 (12-ounce) block silken tofu

⅔ cup water

⅓ cup olive oil

⅓ cup barbecue sauce

2 teaspoons hot sauce

1 teaspoon onion powder

1 teaspoon garlic powder

1 teaspoon seasoning salt

2¼ cups vital wheat gluten

1. Preheat oven to 350°F.

2. Purée the tofu, water, and olive oil for 1 minute. Add the BBQ sauce, hot sauce, onion powder, garlic powder, and seasoning salt.

3. Place mixture in a bowl. Add the vital wheat gluten and form a dough by kneading with your hands. Knead until dough is universally smooth. Let sit for a few minutes and knead again for 2 minutes.

4. Press into loaf pan greased with a little vegan margarine. Bake for 40 minutes. Cut and serve.

# "Chickeny" Seitan

Serves 8

If you add in vegetarian chicken bouillon cubes, seitan will take on a "chicken-like" flavor. It's perfect for when you're craving a meal of chicken but are still in the mood to stick to your vegan guns.

1 cup vital wheat gluten

1 tablespoon nutritional yeast

½ teaspoon dried sage

½ teaspoon thyme

½ teaspoon garlic powder

½ teaspoon onion powder

6 cups plus ¾ cup vegetable broth (or vegetarian chicken-flavor broth/bouillon)

1. Mix the wheat gluten, nutritional yeast, sage, thyme, garlic powder, and onion powder in a medium bowl.

2. Add the ¾ cup of broth to the mix and combine with hands. Knead mixture into a smooth dough. Let sit for a few minutes and knead again for 2 minutes.

3. Divide into 4 pieces, each ½" thick.

4. In a stock pot on low, heat the 6 cups of broth. Add the dough pieces. Simmer them for 1 hour. Use this seitan in Not-Chicken Soup (see Chapter 6 for recipe), or on top of a salad.

# Seitan Buffalo Wings

Serves 4

Buffalo sauce is the most delicious thing on the earth. On the whole entire earth. Buffalos themselves may be a little confused, but that doesn't particularly matter at this juncture. These wings are spicy and the ideal snack while watching (insert Massively Important Game in Sport of Choice here). Serve with Dairy-Free Ranch Dressing (see Chapter 4)!

⅓ cup vegan margarine

⅓ cup Louisiana hot sauce

1 cup flour

1 teaspoon garlic powder

1 teaspoon onion powder

¼ teaspoon pepper

½ cup soy milk

1 (16-ounce) package seitan

Canola oil for frying

1. In a small saucepan over low heat, add the margarine and hot sauce. Stir till the margarine is melted. Set buffalo sauce aside.

2. In a small bowl, combine the flour, garlic powder, onion powder, and pepper. Pour the soy milk in another bowl.

3. Dip the seitan in the soy milk, then the flour mixture.

4. In a deep saucepan over medium heat, heat the oil. Then deep-fry the seitan in the oil until brown for 5 minutes, making sure to cook all sides.

5. When all of the pieces of seitan are cooked, cover them in the buffalo sauce, dip in your homemade ranch dressing and go to town!

# Tandoori Seitan

Serves 6

A classic Indian dish with a vegan twist. Full of such bright and spicy flavors, one bite might make you break out into song like a Bollywood star!

⅔ cup plain soy yogurt

2 tablespoons lemon juice

1½ tablespoons Tandoori spice blend

½ teaspoon cumin

½ teaspoon garlic powder

¼ teaspoon salt

1 (16-ounce) package seitan, chopped

1 onion, chopped

1 yellow bell pepper, chopped

1 tomato, chopped

2 tablespoons oil

1. Whisk up the soy yogurt, lemon juice, and all spices in a bowl. Add in the seitan and let it marinate for an hour. Drain the seitan and reserve the remaining marinade for a topping later.

2. In a large skillet over medium-high heat, sauté the onion, pepper, and tomato in oil for 2 minutes. Reduce heat to low and add the seitan. Cook for 10 minutes, tossing every few minutes.

3. Top with remaining marinade and serve with rice.

# Greek Seitan Gyro

**Serves 6**

You can now make this delicious street food specialty right in your kitchen. Enjoy with pita chips and hummus, or grape leaves and tabouleh salad. Go Greek for a day. Lounge around naked and pretend you're a god. Just don't walk around the neighborhood or anything. Or at least don't blame me if you do. But it would be funny.

¾ teaspoon paprika

½ teaspoon parsley

¼ teaspoon garlic powder

¼ teaspoon oregano

Salt and pepper to taste

1 (16-ounce) package seitan, thinly sliced

2 tablespoons oil

6 pitas

1 tomato, sliced thin

1 onion, chopped

½ head of lettuce, shredded

½ cup nondairy sour cream

1. In a small bowl, mix together paprika, parsley, garlic powder, oregano, salt, and pepper. Coat seitan in the spices.

2. In a medium skillet over medium-low heat, sauté the seitan. Cook for 7 minutes until seitan is browned.

3. Top each pita with the seitan, tomato, onion, lettuce, and nondairy sour cream.

# Super-Meaty TVP Meatloaf

Serves 6

TVP stands for "textured vegetable protein" or soy protein "meat"—slightly unappealing, I know. However, I promise you that this recipe does meatloaf justice. Wow, that's the first time I ever had to stand up for meatloaf. Plus, it's low in fat! This delicious recipe will yet again surprise your tongue with the tasty flexibility of veganism.

2 cups TVP

1¾ cups hot vegetable broth

1 onion

1 tablespoon canola oil

¼ cup ketchup

½ cup plus 3 tablespoons barbecue sauce

1 cup vital wheat gluten

1 cup bread crumbs

1 teaspoon dried parsley

½ teaspoon sage

½ teaspoon salt

¼ teaspoon pepper

1. In a medium bowl, combine TVP with hot vegetable broth to rehydrate. Let sit for 6–7 minutes. Squeeze out the excess moisture when it's through.

2. In a small saucepan over medium heat, sauté the onion in oil for about 4 minutes, until it become clear.

3. Preheat oven to 400°F.

4. In a bowl, mix the TVP, sautéed onion, ketchup, and ½ cup barbecue sauce. After that's mixed properly, add the vital wheat gluten, bread crumbs, and the spices.

5. Press the mix into a loaf pan greased with vegan margarine (don't forget), and pour the remaining 3 tablespoons of barbecue sauce over the top. Cook for 45 minutes. Allow to cool for 10 minutes before attempting to cut. Yay! Serve with baked potatoes and some broccoli.

## THE SKINNY ON ... TVP

TVP comes dehydrated, so it requires that you rehydrate it before usage. Don't worry, this doesn't take long: only about 6 minutes. Believe me, if it took longer that that I would be acting all fussy and whining around the kitchen and never doing it again. Never fear! That's our motto.

# TVP "Sloppy Joes"

Serves 8

Kids love these Sloppy Joes. Nor do they have any idea they are eating yummy sandwiches full of vegany goodness. Ah, kids. Little blank balls of unmolded dough.

1¾ cups TVP

1 cup hot water

1 onion, chopped

1 green bell pepper, diced

2 tablespoons olive oil

1 (16-ounce) can tomato sauce

¼ cup barbecue sauce

2 tablespoons chili powder

1 tablespoon mustard powder

1 tablespoon soy sauce

2 tablespoons molasses

2 tablespoons apple cider vinegar

1 teaspoon hot sauce

1 teaspoon garlic powder

½ teaspoon salt

1. In a medium bowl, mix the TVP with hot water. Let sit for 6 minutes, and then drain.

2. Sauté the onion and bell pepper in the olive oil in a stock pot on medium-high heat for 3 minutes.

3. Reduce heat to medium-low and add the TVP plus all remaining ingredients. Cover and let simmer for 15 minutes. Check back occasionally and stir. Serve on bulky whole wheat rolls with zucchini fries (see recipe in Chapter 2)!

# Sinless TVP Chili "Cheese" Fries

Serves 4

Oh, it's soooo tough being a vegan. Vegans can't eat anything. Except chili cheese fries.

1 (20-ounce) bag frozen French fries

1½ cups TVP

2 cups hot water to rehydrate TVP

½ onion, chopped

1 tablespoon olive oil

1 (15-ounce) can kidney beans

1½ cups tomato paste

2 tablespoons chili powder

½ teaspoon cumin

½ teaspoon cayenne pepper

2 tablespoons vegan margarine

2 tablespoons flour

1½ cups soy milk

2 tablespoons prepared mustard

½ teaspoon garlic powder

½ teaspoon salt

½ cup grated vegan cheese

1. Prepare the French fries using the instructions on the packaging. Don't go wild just yet.

2. Rehydrate TVP by combining it with 2 cups hot water. Let sit for 7 minutes, and then drain.

3. In a medium saucepan over medium heat, cook the onion in the olive oil until translucent. Reduce heat to medium-low and add the beans, TVP, tomato paste, chili powder, cumin, and cayenne pepper. Cover and cook for 10 minutes.

4. In another pot over low heat, melt the vegan margarine and add the flour to form a paste. Add the soy milk, mustard, garlic powder, and salt. Add the vegan cheese and stir in. Heat until everything is cleanly mixed.

5. Top fries with TVP chili, followed by the "cheese" sauce. Sprinkle more "cheese" on top for added aesthetic affect. (Because that's what we look for when we eat chili "cheese" fries.)

# TVP Stuffed Peppers

Serves 6

There is nothing like a warm little pepper piping with protein and goodness. They make a colorful and clever presentation for a hearty meal. Your friends won't miss the sausage!

6 bell peppers

¾ cup TVP

¾ cup hot vegetable broth

1 onion, chopped

2 ribs celery, diced

⅔ cup mushrooms, chopped

2 tablespoons olive oil

1½ cups rice, cooked

1 teaspoon parsley

½ teaspoon oregano

½ teaspoon salt

1½ cups plus ½ cup marinara sauce

1. Preheat oven to 325°F.

2. Cut off the tops of the bell peppers and seed them. Combine the TVP and hot vegetable broth in a small bowl to rehydrate. Let sit for 6–7 minutes. Then drain.

3. In a large saucepan over medium heat, cook the onion, celery, and mushrooms for 5 minutes in the oil until the mushrooms are browned. Reduce heat to medium-low and add the rehydrated TVP, cooked rice, parsley, oregano, salt, and 1½ cups marinara sauce. Heat until mixed well.

4. Stuff the mixture into the peppers and set in a casserole dish. Cover with remaining ½ cup marinara and cook for 30 minutes.

# Baked Mexican Tempeh Cakes

**Serves 4**

This sauce will make tempeh flavorful and perfect, whether you eat it alone or in tacos where you replace carb-laden tortillas with low-cal lettuce leaves as wraps!

2 (8-ounce) packages tempeh

1 cup vegetable broth

½ cup tomato paste

3 cloves garlic, minced

2 tablespoons soy sauce

2 tablespoons apple cider vinegar

3 tablespoons water

1½ teaspoons chili powder

½ teaspoon oregano

¼ teaspoon cayenne pepper

Hot sauce to taste

## PART-TIME TIP

Tempeh can easily absorb sauces and marinades, but remember to simmer the tempeh chunks in water or veggie broth first in order to aid the process.

1. Slice each block of tempeh into 4 pieces.

2. In a medium saucepan over medium-low heat, bring the vegetable broth to a simmer. Then add the tempeh and continue simmering for 10 minutes. Remove and drain.

3. In a small bowl, whisk up the tomato paste, garlic, soy sauce, vinegar, water, chili powder, oregano, and cayenne. Put the tempeh in a shallow dish and cover with the marinade. Allow to marinate for a few hours. The longer you can leave it in, the better! However, I understand. I am inpatient as well.

4. Preheat the oven to 375°F.

5. Move the tempeh into a casserole dish and baste the slices well with the marinade.

6. Bake for about 17 minutes. Turn over, baste again, and cook for another 15 minutes. Top with your choice of veggies, black beans, and hot sauce! *Ay, caramba.*

# Sweet and Sour Tempeh

Serves 4

The enigmatic flavor will leave you both puzzled and pleased. Try some hearty brown rice with this dish to mix with the extra sauce.

1 cup vegetable broth

2 tablespoons soy sauce

1 (8-ounce) package tempeh, diced

2 tablespoons barbecue sauce

2 teaspoons maple syrup

½ teaspoon ground ginger

⅓ cup apple cider vinegar

1 tablespoon cornstarch

1 (15-ounce) can pineapple chunks, divided into chunks and juice

2 tablespoons olive oil

1 yellow bell pepper, chopped

1 red bell pepper, chopped

1 yellow onion, chopped

1. Whisking again! Whisking is fun. Whisk the veggie broth and the soy sauce in a medium saucepan. Set on the stove and let simmer over low heat. Add the tempeh and continue simmering for 10 minutes. Remove the tempeh and strain it, reserving ½ cup of the veggie broth.

2. Whisk! Whisk the BBQ sauce, maple syrup, ginger, vinegar, cornstarch, and pineapple juice in a small bowl. Make sure no clumps remain.

3. In a medium skillet over medium heat, heat the olive oil and toast the tempeh, peppers, and onion for 2 minutes.

4. Add the sauce mixture, and allow to simmer. Let the sauce thicken up, cooking for 8 minutes. Top with the pineapple chunks.

# Crispy Tempeh Fries

**Serves 2**

Absolutely delicious for a snack with marinara sauce, bean dip, or all on their own. I like to put a little nutritional yeast over these, or some melted vegan shredded cheese and fakeon—that is, Fake Bacon. It's not a crime to have a little throwback to the days of meat and fatty cheese every now and then. So kill me! Bacon tastes so good.

1 (8-ounce) package tempeh

½ teaspoon salt

½ teaspoon chili powder

½ teaspoon garlic powder

Canola oil for frying

1. Slice up tempeh into thin strips. Simmer in water for about 10 minutes to soften them up and make them digestible. Drain excess liquid.

2. While the tempeh pieces are still wet, sprinkle them with the salt, chili, and garlic powder.

3. In a medium saucepan, heat oil over medium-low heat. Fry tempeh pieces for 6 minutes in oil until browned and crispy. Let them cool for 30 minutes on a paper towel (to absorb excess oil).

4. After the pieces cool, heat up the oil once more and fry them again for 6 minutes. Double-frying never hurt anyone's taste buds! Season with your choice of spices when warm.

# CHAPTER 13

# Dinner Plans

## BECAUSE NO ONE NEEDS TO KNOW YOU DIDN'T THINK OF IT YOURSELF

All ready for you in your hour of need. I know, you're like me. You're a procrastinator. Let's high-five on that. Tomorrow.

# DINNER PLAN  1

## The Sophisticated Sweet Tooth
SERVES 4

**Appetizer:** Spicy Sweet Cucumber Salad

**Main Course:** Caramelized Onion and
Barbecue Sauce Pizza

**Dessert:** Maple Date Carrot Cake

# Spicy Sweet Cucumber Salad

A cool and refreshing starter to get your mouth ready for the sweet and savory delights to come.

4 cucumbers, thinly sliced

1½ teaspoons salt

½ cup red wine vinegar

2 tablespoons agave nectar

2 teaspoons sesame oil

½ teaspoon red pepper flakes

1 onion, thinly sliced

1.  On a baking sheet, spread out sliced cucumbers and sprinkle with salt. Let sit for 10 minutes. Drain excess water from cucumbers.

2.  Whisk up rice vinegar, agave nectar, oil, and red pepper flakes in a small bowl.

3.  Cover cucumbers with dressing and add onion slices. Toss.

4.  Let sit for 10 minutes before serving so flavors meet and greet.

# Caramelized Onion and Barbecue Sauce Pizza

Sweet, tangy, and packed with protein thanks to tofu. Try making this dish with whole grain pizza dough for an even more filling meal. This recipe will prove how you don't need cheese to make a great pie! Your friends will be impressed that you can turn a pizza into something so elegant. Hell, I'm impressed and I wrote the recipe. You're so much more talented than me.

⅔ cup barbecue sauce

1 vegan pizza crust or pizza dough (almost all are, just check the label)

2 red onions, chopped

3 tablespoons olive oil

1 pound block tofu, diced

½ cup diced pineapple, drained or fresh

⅓ teaspoon garlic powder

Salt and pepper to taste

1. Preheat oven to 450°F. Spread barbecue sauce over the pizza crust. If you bought a premade-crust, simply put it onto the oven rack as is. If you purchased dough, lightly grease a pan with vegan margarine and smooth the dough inside.

2. In a medium skillet over medium heat, sauté onions in olive oil for a good 4 minutes. Add the tofu, and continue cooking until the tofu is crisped and the onions are translucent.

3. Top the pizza with all ingredients. Sprinkle with the garlic powder and be generous with the salt and pepper.

4. Bake for approximately 14 minutes. You will know the pizza is done when the bottom is lightly browned.

# Maple Date Carrot Cake

A moist cake that would go great with a little vegan frosting (see From Scratch Chocolate Cake with Vanilla Frosting recipe later in this chapter). The pineapple juice in this recipe ties in subtly to the main course's diced pineapple topping. Very keen of you, linking them like that. Very clever. This serves 4, and then everyone can have another piece. How fab is that?

1½ cups raisins

1⅓ cups pineapple juice

6 dates, diced

2¼ cups grated carrot

½ cup maple syrup

¼ cup applesauce

2 tablespoons oil

3 cups flour

1½ teaspoons baking soda

½ teaspoon salt

1 teaspoon cinnamon

½ teaspoon allspice

Egg-replacement mixture, the equivalent of 2 eggs, prepared according to package directions

## PART-TIME TIP

To make the dates or other dried fruits smoother for blending or baking, always soak them first in water, for about 15 minutes. It's fine if you skip this step, but you may get little chunks of date here and there if you don't.

1. Preheat oven to 350°F. Grease with vegan margarine and flour a 9" cake pan.

2. In a small bowl, mix raisins with pineapple juice and let sit for 10 minutes. In another dish, soak the dates in water for 10 minutes and then drain.

3. In a large bowl, mix up the raisins, pineapple juice, dates, carrot, maple syrup, applesauce, and oil. In another bowl, mix the flour, baking soda, salt, cinnamon, and allspice. The word *allspice* sounds so fun, doesn't it? It's like a party for all spices. I imagine it to be a great time.

4. Mix the wet and dry ingredients together. Add the egg-replacement mix.

5. Pour the batter in the cake pan (well, it isn't going to fly there itself), and bake for 30 minutes. Use the old toothpick trick before taking it out of the oven: Make sure the toothpick comes out clean from the center of the cake.

# DINNER PLAN  2

## The Mama Mia
SERVES 4

**Appetizer:** White Bean and Orzo Minestrone

**Main Course:** Breaded Eggplant "Parmesan"

**Dessert:** Cocoa-Nut-Coconut No-Bake Cookies

# White Bean and Orzo Minestrone

**Makes 6 servings**

A delicious traditional soup full of veggies, pasta, and delicious hearty beans. A classic. Light a candle and put on some romantic accordion music. When in Rome . . . as they say.

3 cloves garlic, minced

1 onion, chopped

2 ribs celery, chopped

2 tablespoons olive oil

5 cups vegetable broth

1 carrot, diced

1 cup green beans, chopped

2 small potatoes, diced

2 tomatoes, chopped

1 (15-ounce) can cannellini beans, drained

1 teaspoon basil

½ teaspoon oregano

¾ cup orzo

Salt and pepper to taste

1. In a large stock pot over medium heat, sauté the garlic, onion, and celery in the olive oil for 4 minutes.

2. Add the veggie broth. Add the carrot, green beans, potatoes, tomatoes, beans, basil, and oregano. Bring to a simmer. Cover and cook on medium-low for 25 minutes.

3. Add the orzo. Cook another 10 minutes, uncovered, and season with salt and pepper.

# Breaded Eggplant "Parmesan"

A favorite of vegans and non-vegans alike. The perfect complement to your presentation Italiano. The *pièce de résistance.* The Sistine Chapel to your glorious catalogue. I'm exaggerating a little. It's the Italian thing to do, after all.

1 medium eggplant

½ teaspoon salt

¾ cup flour

1 teaspoon garlic powder

⅔ cup soy milk

Egg-replacement mixture, the equivalent of 2 eggs, prepared according to package directions

1½ cups bread crumbs

2 tablespoons Italian seasonings

¼ cup nutritional yeast

1½ cups marinara sauce

1 (8-ounce) package of vegan "mozzarella" cheese (optional)

1. Slice up the eggplant into ¾"-thick pieces and sprinkle with salt. Let sit for 10 minutes and drain of excess moisture.

2. Set up 3 bowls. In the first, mix flour and garlic powder. In the second, whisk up soy milk and egg-replacer. In the third, mix the bread crumbs, Italian seasoning, and nutritional yeast.

3. Coat the eggplant pieces with the flour mix, then gently dip in the soy milk mix, and lastly dredge in the bread crumb mix. Place onto a greased casserole dish.

4. Bake for 25 minutes. Remove from oven, cover in marinara sauce, and bake for another 5 minutes. If you wish, when you remove the eggplant from the oven the first time, top with your favorite vegan "mozzarella cheese."

# Cocoa-Nut-Coconut No-Bake Cookies

**Makes 2 dozen cookies**

It wouldn't be an Italian Christmas without bite-sized macaroon cookies. This veganized version of a well-known favorite will have you grinning with delight, and perhaps even speaking some words *d'amore* to your neighbor. (So make sure you're sitting next to someone you like, or it could get pretty awkward.)

¼ cup vegan margarine

½ cup soy milk

2 cups sugar

⅓ cup cocoa

½ cup nut butter (almond butter works best)

½ teaspoon vanilla

3 cups quick-cooking oats

½ cup almonds, finely chopped

½ cup coconut flakes

1. Line a baking sheet with waxed paper.

2. In a large saucepan over low heat, heat the vegan margarine and soy milk until the margarine has melted. Add the sugar and cocoa. Stir and bring to a boil in order to dissolve the sugar. Reduce heat to low and add in the nut butter, cooking until it's melted.

3. Remove from heat and add in all other ingredients.

4. Spoon out little balls of the mixture onto the wax paper using a spoon, and press them into a cookie shape. Chill until firm, about 2 hours.

# DINNER PLAN  3

## The Ay Caramba
SERVES 4

**Appetizer:** Nacho "Cheese" Dip

**Main Course:** Tofu and Portobello "Enchiladas"

**Dessert:** Coconut Rice Pudding

# Nacho "Cheese" Dip

You won't miss those dubious looking canned and artificial cheese dips once you cook up this delicious recipe. Top with some guacamole, and dip in your favorite tortilla chips. Then, of course, snack away!

3 tablespoons vegan margarine

1 cup unsweetened soy milk

¾ teaspoon onion powder

½ teaspoon garlic powder

½ teaspoon salt

1 tablespoon peanut butter

¼ cup flour

¼ cup nutritional yeast

¾ cup salsa

2 tablespoons chopped jalapenos

1. In a medium saucepan on low, heat margarine and soy milk. Add in the onion powder, garlic powder, and salt. Drop in the peanut butter and stir well until everything is combined.

2. Add the flour into the stovetop mixture one tablespoon at a time. Stir continuously. Everything should thicken up in about 5 minutes.

3. Add the nutritional yeast, salsa, and jalapenos. Remove from heat.

4. The dip will thicken up as it cools off a bit! Serve warm.

Tofu and Portobello "Enchiladas"

The tofu will fill you up, and the portobello mushrooms add a sophisticated flavor. Stuff in some vegan cheese and top with a little hot sauce to get the full effect.

1-pound block firm tofu, diced small

5 portobello mushrooms with gills removed, chopped

1 onion, diced

3 cloves garlic, minced

2 tablespoons oil

2 teaspoons chili powder

½ cup sliced black olives

1 (15-ounce) can enchilada sauce

8–10 flour tortillas (check label to make certain they're vegan)

½ cup vegan cheese

1. Preheat oven to 350°F.

2. In a large skillet over medium heat, cook the tofu, mushrooms, onion, and garlic in the olive oil for five minutes. Add in the chili powder and mix up well, cooking for another minute longer.

3. Take off the heat. Mix in olives and ⅓ cup of the enchilada sauce.

4. Lightly cover the bottom of a casserole dish with more enchilada sauce.

5. Fill each tortilla with ¼ cup mushroom-tofu mixture and roll them up. Fit them snugly in the casserole dish. Top with the leftover enchilada sauce and vegan cheese. Bake 30 minutes.

## PART-TIME TIP

All breads, pizza doughs, and taco shells are typically vegan. However, it's always worth a glance at the ingredients list if you're unsure or you are using a new brand. Sometimes certain taco wraps are made with lard, or certain breads include buttermilk and egg.

# Coconut Rice Pudding

Rice pudding is a traditional Mexican dessert. Try this jazzed-up vegan version as the perfect ending for your dinner menu. *Delicioso!* Your guests will be sure to say *gracias*.

1½ cup vanilla soy milk

1½ cups coconut milk

1½ cups cooked white rice

2 tablespoons maple syrup

2 tablespoons agave nectar

4–5 dates, chopped

Dash cinnamon

2 mangos, chopped

1. In a large saucepan on low heat, mix the soy milk, coconut milk, and rice together. Cook for 10 minutes until mixture thickens.

2. Add the maple syrup, agave nectar, and dates. Cook for another 3 minutes.

3. Remove from heat and let cool for about 5 minutes. Garnish with cinnamon and mangos.

# DINNER PLAN  4

## The Way Easier Than It Should Be
SERVES 4

**Appetizer:** Vegan "Pigs" in a Blanket

**Main Course:** So Incredibly Easy Black Bean Burgers

**Dessert:** Chocolate Chip Cookies

# Vegan "Pigs" in a Blanket

Bite-sized popular appetizers go vegan. So easy to make and perfect alongside spicy mustard or plain old ketchup.

1 batch Down-Home Vegan Biscuits dough (see Chapter 3 for recipe)

8 vegan hot dogs, sliced in half

1.  Preheat oven to 400°F. Lightly grease a cookie sheet with vegan margarine.

2.  Divide up dough into 8 even balls and roll each one out.

3.  Place hot dog into the center of the dough and roll up.

4.  Place on cookie sheet and cook for 12 minutes.

# So Incredibly Easy Black Bean Burgers

**Makes 6 patties**

Simple burgers that don't fall apart. Go along with the easy-summer feel and serve the burgers and vegan "pigs" with lemonade and a easy vegan potato salad.

1 (15-ounce) can black beans, drained

3 tablespoons minced onions

1 teaspoon salt

1½ teaspoons garlic powder

2 teaspoons parsley

1 teaspoon chili powder

⅔ cup flour

Canola oil for frying

1.  Process the black beans in a food processor until partially blended.

2.  Place black beans in a medium bowl. Add in the onions and all spices. Mash up with a fork to combine.

3.  Add the flour in slowly, continuing to mash with a fork. Form into patties.

4.  In a medium skillet over medium heat, add oil. Cook black bean patties for 3 minutes on each side. You don't want them soft on the inside, so make certain to cook them for the full 6 minutes.

# Chocolate Chip Cookies

**Makes 2 dozen cookies**

The classic. But you know, healthier, tastier, and all around better in every way.

⅔ cup vegan margarine

⅔ cup sugar

⅔ cup brown sugar

⅓ cup applesauce

1½ teaspoon vanilla

Egg-replacement mixture, the equivalent of 2 eggs, prepared according to package directions

2½ cups flour

1 teaspoon baking soda

½ teaspoon baking powder

1 teaspoon salt

⅔ cup quick-cooking rolled oats

1½ cups vegan chocolate or carob chips

1. Preheat oven to 375°F.

2. Cream together margarine and white sugar. Add brown sugar, applesauce, vanilla, and egg-replacer. Mix well.

3. In another bowl, mix the flour, baking soda, baking powder, and salt.

4. Combine wet and dry ingredients. Mix well.

5. Stir in oats and chocolate chips until evenly dispersed through the dough.

6. Use a spoon to drop little balls of dough onto a very lightly greased cookie sheet. Bake for 12 minutes.

# DINNER PLAN  5

## The Anytime Thanksgiving
SERVES 4

**Appetizer:** Cashew Cream of Asparagus Soup

**Main Course:** Sweet Stuffed Butternut Squash

**Dessert:** Ginger Spice Cookies

# Cashew Cream of Asparagus Soup

Filling, tasty, and hearty, this low-calorie soup packs 10 grams of protein thanks to delicious cashew nuts. This unexpected combination melds perfectly for a hot soup that is ace for dipping warm pieces of garlic bread. You'll certainly have something to be thankful for this faux-Thanksgiving.

1 onion, chopped

4 cloves garlic, minced

2 tablespoons olive oil

2 pounds asparagus, trimmed and chopped

4 cups vegetable broth

¾ cup raw cashews

¾ cup water

¼ teaspoon dried sage

½ teaspoon salt

¼ teaspoon black pepper

2 teaspoons lemon juice

2 tablespoons nutritional yeast

1. In a large pot on medium-high, sauté the onion and garlic in the oil. Cook for about 3 minutes. Add the asparagus and vegetable broth.

2. Bring to a simmer, and cover. Cook for 20 minutes and then transfer the mixture to a food processor. Process until nearly smooth and put back on the stovetop.

3. Purée the cashews and water in the food processor. Add this to the stovetop mixture. Add in the sage, salt, and pepper.

4. Lastly, add in the lemon juice and nutritional yeast for a flavorful pop. Serve with garlic bread.

# Sweet Stuffed Butternut Squash

Some people love sweet potatoes, but butternut squash has stolen my heart (and stomach). It manages to be sweet and soft without getting mushy, as potatoes sometimes become. Yet another easy and nutritional recipe to add to your already stellar repertoire.

2 small butternut squash

½ cup apple juice

2 apples, diced

½ cup chopped pecans

⅓ cup dried cranberries

¼ cup maple syrup

2 tablespoons vegan margarine, melted

½ teaspoon cinnamon

¼ teaspoon nutmeg

## PART-TIME TIP

Don't like cranberries? Use dried blueberries or raisins. Hate tofu? Try the dish with seitan. Despise celery? Add in asparagus. Not a fan of soy milk? Use hemp milk. The beauty of cooking is the literally endless list of possibilities you can create using your own preferences and imagination. There's no shame in deconstructing a presented recipe and creating something entirely new! Sometimes, just substituting one spice for another can make a monumental difference in the taste of a dish. Cooking is not only an art, but a science! So apply the scientific method: experiment and observe. (And eat, duh.)

1. Preheat the oven to 350°F. Peel the butternut squash, slice in half lengthwise, and scrape out the seeds.

2. Pour the apple juice into a nonstick baking sheet with a lip and place the squash onto the sheet cut side up. Roast for 20 minutes in the oven. If you want, brush a little olive oil onto the squash as well.

3. In a bowl, mix the apples, pecans, and cranberries. Add the maple syrup, vegan margarine, cinnamon, and nutmeg. Stir well.

4. Stuff the squash with the filling and roast for another 25 minutes.

# Ginger Spice Cookies

**Makes 18 cookies**

It wouldn't be the holidays without a little ginger thrown in. It's an ingredient that seems to hearken back all those memories of warm family get-togethers with laughter and cider and whiskey all a-flow. You don't need to add the whiskey to your shindig, of course, but it certainly helps.

⅓ cup vegan margarine

½ cup maple syrup

⅓ cup molasses

¼ cup almond milk

2¼ cups flour

1 teaspoon baking powder

½ teaspoon baking soda

½ teaspoon cinnamon

½ teaspoon ginger

¼ teaspoon allspice

½ teaspoon salt

1. Cream the vegan margarine, maple syrup, molasses, and almond milk.

2. In a different bowl, mix the flour, baking powder, baking soda, cinnamon, ginger, allspice, and salt.

3. Mix the wet and dry ingredients together. Chill in the fridge for about 30 minutes.

4. Roll up the dough into little 1½" balls. (I always taste the batter of vegan desserts—no raw eggs, no harm!) Place them on a cookie sheet greased with vegan margarine and pat them down a bit so they don't cook in perfect little circles. Bake for 350°F about 12 minutes. Keep an eye on them so the bottoms don't burn! Serve alongside some creamy vanilla soy ice cream.

# DINNER PLAN  6

## The Zen Moment
SERVES 4

**Appetizer:** Udon Noodle Buddha Bowl

**Main Course:** Sesame Baked Tofu

**Dessert:** Apricot Ginger Sorbet

# Udon Noodle Buddha Bowl

This soup, full of chewy udon noodles, is yummy as an appetizer and cooks in a snap.

2 (8-ounce) packages udon noodles, cooked and drained

3½ cups Shiitake and Garlic Broth (see recipe in Chapter 6)

1½ teaspoons fresh ginger, minced

1 tablespoon sugar

1 tablespoon soy sauce

1 tablespoon rice vinegar

¼ teaspoon red pepper flakes

1 baby bok choy, chopped

1 cup mushrooms, any kind, chopped

1 pound block silken tofu, cubed

¼ cup bean sprouts

1 cup fresh spinach

1 teaspoon sesame oil

1. Place equal amounts of the cooked noodles into four serving bowls. Unless, of course, you plan on being selfish.

2. On the stovetop in a big ol' pot over medium heat, combine the Shiitake and Garlic Broth, ginger, sugar, soy sauce, vinegar, and red pepper flakes. Bring the broth to a simmer and add the baby bok choy, mushrooms, and tofu. Let these puppies cook for a good 10 minutes.

3. Next, add the bean sprouts and spinach and continue to simmer for another minute. Drizzle the soup with sesame oil after taking it off the stove, and divide it equally into the bowls with the noodles.

# Sesame Baked Tofu

**Makes 6 servings**

A meaty and deliciously flavorful dish. Serve atop a nice big plate of steamed brown rice with peas and bamboo shoots. You don't need a cookie to know your fortune this time: Your guests are going to love it.

¼ cup soy sauce

2 tablespoons sesame oil

¾ teaspoon garlic powder

½ teaspoon ginger powder

2 (1 pound) blocks extra-firm tofu, well pressed

3–4 tablespoons sesame seeds

1. In a small bowl, whisk the soy sauce, sesame oil, garlic powder, and ginger powder.

2. Slice the tofu into 1½" pieces and place them in a shallow dish. Add the marinade. Let sit for an least 1 hour.

3. Preheat oven to 400°F. Coat a cookie sheet with olive oil, and place pieces of tofu on top.

4. Bake for 25 minutes. Turn over and bake for another 10 minutes.

5. Toss tofu in sesame seeds to coat. Serve over rice!

# Apricot Ginger Sorbet

A divine ending for your culinary trip. Cool, sweet, and healthy. Hardly any fat and complemented by chunks of fresh fruit.

⅔ cup water

⅔ cup sugar

2 teaspoons fresh minced ginger

5 cups chopped apricots

3 tablespoons lemon juice

1. In a large saucepan over medium heat, cook the water, sugar, and ginger. Bring to a boil, and then lower the heat to a simmer. Cook for another 4 minutes until the sugar transforms into a syrup. Fancy, eh? Let cool.

2. Purée the cooked syrup with the apricots and lemon juice.

3. Pour into a freezer-safe dish and freeze. Stir every 30 minutes for 4 hours. It's a pain, but hey, sorbet is worth a little work, right? Four hours later, your sorbet is ready-Freddy.

# DINNER PLAN  7

## The Quite Right and Proper Dinner
SERVES 6

**Appetizer:** Vegan Cheese Ball

**Main Course:** No Shepherd, No Sheep Pie

**Dessert:** Tofu Chocolate Pudding

# Vegan Cheese Ball

**Makes 1 large cheese ball or 14 bite-sized cheese balls**

Serve with delicate little crackers for a truly elegant display. It will be ever-so lovely. Do remember to give yourself a pat on the back. Good show! By George. Carry on!

1 (8-ounce) block vegan cheddar cheese, room temperature

1 (12-ounce) container vegan cream cheese

1 teaspoon garlic powder

½ teaspoon hot sauce

¼ teaspoon salt

1 teaspoon paprika

¼ cup nuts, finely chopped (walnuts work great)

1. Process vegan cheese using the "grate" tool until finely grated, or simply use a hand-held cheese grater. Mash the grated cheese together with the vegan cream cheese, garlic powder, hot sauce, and salt.

2. Chill for at least 1 hour until firm. Shape into a log. Sprinkle with paprika and roll into the nuts. Serve with little crackers and some tea. Or a nice English stout. Beer definitely works too.

# No Shepherd, No Sheep Pie

There is absolutely nothing more comforting on this earth than a nice, hot, steaming slice of shepherd's pie. It will warm your guests to their very toes and heat the heart for lively discussions of the jovial nature.

1½ cups TVP

1½ cups hot vegetable broth

½ onion, chopped

2 cloves garlic, minced

1 large carrot, sliced thin

2 tablespoons olive oil

¾ cup sliced mushrooms

½ cup green peas

½ cup veggie broth

½ cup plus 3 tablespoons soy milk

1 tablespoon flour

5 medium potatoes, cooked

2 tablespoons vegan margarine

¼ teaspoon rosemary

½ teaspoon sage

½ teaspoon salt

¼ teaspoon black pepper

1. Preheat oven to 350°F.

2. In a medium bowl, mix TVP with 1½ cups hot veggie broth and let sit for 6 minutes. Drain.

3. In a medium skillet over medium-high heat, sauté the onion, garlic, and carrot in the olive oil for 5 minutes. Then add the mushrooms, peas, ½ cup veggie broth, and ½ cup soy milk. Add the flour, letting the sauce thicken up. Then move the mixture into a casserole dish.

4. In a large bowl, mash the potatoes, margarine, and the 3 tablespoons soy milk with the rosemary, sage, salt, and pepper. Spread over the veggies in the casserole pan. Starting to look good, isn't it?

5. Bake for 35 minutes. Enjoy, mate!

# Tofu Chocolate Pudding

The English do love their puddings, don't they? *Pudding* in the English sense can mean anything from a small moist cake, to a custard, to a rice pudding. It's a pretty loose term, so there is certainly space for a delicious you'll-never-guess-it-was-tofu dish.

3 (1 pound) blocks silken tofu

¾ cup cocoa powder

1½ teaspoons vanilla

¾ cup peanut butter, or any other nut butter

¾ cup maple syrup

½ cup raisins for garnish

Process all ingredients (except raisins) until smooth and creamy. You may want to do this in two separate batches so you don't overload your food processor. Serve, sprinkling with raisins.

# DINNER PLAN  8

## The Backyard BBQ Wannabe
SERVES 6

**Appetizer:** Tempeh Dill "Chicken" Salad

**Main Course:** Seitan Barbecue "Meat"

**Dessert:** Chocolate Graham Cracker Candy Bars

# Tempeh Dill "Chicken" Salad

What would a backyard barbecue be without chicken salad? What would Captain Kirk be without Mr. Spock? What would the Internet be without time to waste? Nothing. That's the answer. Nothing at all.

2 (8-ounce) packages tempeh, diced small

Water for boiling

6 tablespoons vegan mayonnaise

2 tablespoons lemon juice

½ teaspoon garlic powder

1 teaspoon Dijon mustard

2 tablespoons sweet pickle relish

½ cup green peas

2 stalks celery, diced small

1 tablespoon fresh chopped dill

1. In a medium saucepan over medium-low heat, combine tempeh and water and let simmer for 10 minutes. Drain.

2. Whisk up the mayo, lemon juice, garlic powder, Dijon, and relish.

3. In a large bowl, mix the drained tempeh, the mayo mixture, peas, celery, and dill. Toss the salad, because you must *toss* a salad. What else could you do to it? Mix? That's dull.

4. Chill for an hour, and serve!

PROTEIN
QUICK
FLEX

# Seitan Barbecue "Meat"

Have the winter blues and wish you were lazily hanging out on your porch in July? Sadly, you can't change the weather, but you can always change up some flavors to pretend you're living in a summertime wonderland. A little delusion never hurt anybody. (Not speaking from experience or anything . . . .)

1 package prepared seitan, sliced into thin strips (about 2 cups)

1 large onion, chopped

3 cloves garlic, minced

2 tablespoons oil

1 cup barbecue sauce

2 tablespoons water

6 sourdough bread rolls, toasted

1 head of lettuce, shredded

1 tomato, sliced

Vegan mayo to taste (see Chapter 4 for recipe)

1. In a medium saucepan over medium-low heat, heat the seitan, onion, and garlic in the oil. Stir continuously for about 4 minutes.

2. Reduce heat to medium-low and add in the BBQ sauce and water. Let simmer and stir frequently for 10 minutes.

3. Fill each roll with even parts BBQ seitan, lettuce, tomato, and vegan mayo!

# Chocolate Graham Cracker Candy Bars

**Makes 16 bars**

Melty, gooey, delicious, and easy. Pretty much the recipe for SUCCESS, in capital letters.

1 cup almond butter, or other nut butter

8 vegan graham crackers, quartered

1 cup vegan chocolate chips

¼ cup vegan margarine

½ cup coconut flakes

¼ cup chopped walnuts

1. Line a baking sheet with waxed paper.

2. Spread about 1 tablespoon almond butter on each cracker and top with another to make a sandwich.

3. On very low heat, melt the chocolate chips and the margarine together in a small saucepan.

4. Using tongs, dip each "cracker sandwich" into the melted chips, and cover the sandwiches. Set them back on the baking sheet and sprinkle them with coconut and nuts.

5. Chill until firm, about 1 hour. Gobble up and send guests home with leftovers (or be greedy and keep them all to yourself)!

# DINNER PLAN  9

## The How Is This Not a Million Calories?
SERVES 4

**Appetizer:** Classic Green Bean Casserole

**Main Course:** TVP, Mushroom, and White Wine Stroganoff

**Dessert:** Foolproof Vegan Fudge

# Classic Green Bean Casserole

Everyone likes a little veggies with their fried onions. Er, or wait. Shouldn't that be the other way around? Well. Nobody will be asking questions when the dish tastes this good.

1 (12-ounce) bag of frozen green beans

¾ cup sliced mushrooms

2 tablespoons vegan margarine

2 tablespoons flour

1½ cups soy milk

1 tablespoon Dijon mustard

½ teaspoon garlic powder

½ teaspoon salt

¼ teaspoon parsley

⅓ teaspoon oregano

¼ teaspoon black pepper

1½ cups French-fried onions

1. Preheat oven to 375°F. Place green beans and mushrooms in a large casserole dish.

2. In a small saucepan over low heat, melt margarine and add in flour until a paste forms. Add the soy milk, mustard, garlic powder, salt, parsley, oregano, and pepper. Stir.

3. Pour the sauce over the mushrooms and green beans, topping with the French-fried onions. Bake for 18 minutes until toasted.

# TVP, Mushroom, and White Wine Stroganoff

A stroganoff is a creamy and rich Russian dish typically served over potatoes, pasta, or rice. Serve yours however you like—just don't forget the vodka cocktails.

¾ cup TVP

¾ cup hot vegetable broth

1 onion, diced

1½ cups sliced mushrooms

2 tablespoons vegan margarine

½ cup white wine

½ teaspoon sage

½ teaspoon parsley

½ teaspoon garlic powder

1 tablespoon flour

2 cups soy milk

½ cup nondairy sour cream

2 tablespoons Dijon mustard

Salt and pepper to taste

1. In a small bowl, mix the TVP and hot veggie broth to rehydrate. Let sit for about 7 minutes. Drain.

2. In a large skillet over medium heat, cook the onion and mushrooms in the margarine for about 2 minutes. Add the white wine, sage, parsley, and garlic powder. Simmer for 4 minutes on medium-low.

3. Add in the flour and stir continuously so the sauce gets a thick consistency.

4. Slowly add in the soy milk, whisking to combine. Heat until sauce is thick.

5. Next, add the nondairy sour cream and Dijon mustard. Stir until well combined. Combine with TVP. Season with salt and pepper.

# Foolproof Vegan Fudge

**Makes two dozen 1" pieces**

Rich and delicious, vegan fudge is just as good as the "real" stuff. So good, actually, that no one will ever know the difference. See, a little fraud may or may not be a good thing!

½ cup vegan margarine

⅓ cup cocoa

⅓ cup soy cream

½ teaspoon vanilla

2 tablespoons peanut butter

3–3½ cups powdered sugar

¾ cup nuts, finely chopped

1. Grease an 8"×8" square baking dish with vegan margarine.

2. In a medium saucepan on very low heat, melt the margarine, cocoa, soy cream, vanilla, and peanut butter. Yum.

3. Add in powdered sugar little by little until the mixture is thick. Add the nuts.

4. Quickly transfer the mixture into the greased pan and chill for 2 hours. Wait until completely firm to cut and serve. *Voila*!

# DINNER PLAN ⏺ 10

## The Comfort Food Feast (or, "Like How Mom Used to Make")
SERVES 6

**Appetizer:** Strawberry Milkshakes

**Main Course:** "Cheesy" Macaroni and "Hamburger" Casserole

**Dessert:** From Scratch Chocolate Cake with Vanilla Icing

# Strawberry Milkshakes

Who can resist a sweet treat before dinner? A direct throwback to childhood afternoons. That is, um, if you can still remember childhood. It wasn't *that* long ago. That's our story, and we're sticking to it.

1½ cups frozen strawberries

1½ (1 pound) blocks silken tofu

1 banana

¾ cup apple juice

6 scoops vanilla soy ice cream

3 tablespoons maple syrup

12 ice cubes

Blend all ingredients, except ice cream, together. Pour into tall glasses and top each with 1 scoop ice cream.

# "Cheesy" Macaroni and "Hamburger" Casserole

No one can forget those boxed favorites mom used to pull out of the cupboard and cook up. On special nights, I'd be allowed to sit in front of the TV with a bowl of macaroni and watch my favorite adventure movies. (You're the best, Mom.)

1 (12-ounce) box elbow macaroni

4 veggie burgers thawed and crumbled, or 1 (12-ounce) package vegetarian "beef" crumbles

1 tomato, diced

1 tablespoon olive oil

1 tablespoon chili powder

1 cup soy milk

2 tablespoons vegan margarine

2 tablespoons flour

1 teaspoon garlic powder

1 teaspoon onion powder

¼ cup nutritional yeast

Salt and pepper to taste

1. Prepare macaroni according to instructions on package.

2. In a large skillet over medium-low heat, cook veggie burgers and tomato in olive oil. Sauté until the veggie burgers are lightly browned. Season with chili powder.

3. In another pan on low heat, heat the soy milk and margarine. Stir together until well mixed. Slowly add the flour to thicken up the sauce. Then, add in the garlic powder, onion powder, and nutritional yeast.

4. Combine macaroni, sauce, and veggie burgers. Season with salt and pepper and serve warm!

# From Scratch Chocolate Cake with Vanilla Frosting

Um, hold the phone. Heavy, dense, and delicious, this vegan chocolate cake is just as good if not better than "normal" chocolate cake. And you can bet your virtue on that.

1½ cups whole wheat flour

¾ cup sugar

⅓ cup dark cocoa powder

1 teaspoon baking soda

1 cup soy milk

¼ cup applesauce

2 tablespoons oil

1 tablespoon vinegar

1 teaspoon vanilla

1. Preheat oven to 350°F. Grease a round 9" cake pan.

2. Mix the flour, sugar, cocoa, and baking soda in a bowl.

3. In another bowl, mix the soy milk, applesauce, oil, vinegar, and vanilla.

4. Combine the wet and dry mixtures. Pour into pan and cook for about 28 minutes. Test with a toothpick in the center of the cake. If it comes out clean, you're all set.

5. Let cool before drizzling with icing and topping with fresh berries.

**To Make Vanilla Icing**

¼ cup soy milk

⅓ cup vegan margarine

2 teaspoons vanilla

3½ cups powdered sugar

1. To make icing, combine all ingredients in the food processor, adding powdered sugar last.

**THE** SKINNY **ON . . . Egg-Replacer**

When cooking, if you're just looking to keep things moist, you need not use egg-replacer. Try out applesauce, soy yogurt, jam, preserves, or even hummus! Be creative. It's sexy.

# DINNER PLAN  11

## The Easygoing Mediterranean
SERVES 4

**Appetizer:** Eggplant Baba Ghanoush

**Main Course:** Easy Falafel Patties

**Dessert:** Easy Banana Date Cookies

# Eggplant Baba Ghanoush

A traditional Arabic spread, this dip will be an adventure for those who've never tried it. Creamy with a tang, it's the perfect topper for pita bread or buttery crackers.

2 medium eggplants

3 tablespoons olive oil, divided

2 tablespoons lemon juice

¼ cup tahini

3 cloves garlic

½ teaspoon cumin

½ teaspoon chili powder

¼ teaspoon salt

1 tablespoon chopped fresh parsley

1. Preheat oven to 400°F. Slice eggplants in half and prick with a fork a bunch of times.

2. Drizzle with 1 tablespoon oil, and then bake eggplant for 30 minutes on a baking sheet.

3. Remove the insides and place in a bowl. Mash all ingredients together. Serve warm.

# Easy Falafel Patties

Falafel is both scrumptious and filling. Make mouthwatering sandwiches with falafel patties, lettuce, tomato, a little hummus, and tahini.

1 (15-ounce) can chick peas, drained

½ onion, minced

1 tablespoon flour

1 teaspoon cumin

¾ teaspoon garlic powder

¾ teaspoon salt

¼ teaspoon paprika

Egg-replacement mixture, the equivalent of 1 egg, prepared according to package directions

¼ cup chopped fresh parsley

2 tablespoons chopped fresh cilantro

1. Preheat oven to 375°F.

2. Pulse chick peas in the food processor until finely chopped.

3. Add flour, cumin, garlic powder, onion, salt, paprika, and egg substitute. Pulse. Add the parsley and cilantro.

4. Shape batter into patties and bake for 15 minutes on a greased cookie sheet, turning over once.

## Easy Bana

**Makes 1 dozen**

Whenever I think of Middle Ea
packed with sweet sugary goo
similar to this is eaten in the I

1 cup chopped pitted dates
1 banana
½ teaspoon vanilla
1¾ cups coconut flakes
¼ cup chopped almonds

cook for 12 minutes. Ea
and chewy and warm.

# CHAPTER 14

# Sinful Desserts

Count your vegan blessings.

# Strawberry Coconut Ice Cream

Serves 6

Luscious, rich, and everything that ice cream should be. Oh, except the bad-for-you part.

2 cups coconut cream

1¾ cups frozen strawberries

¾ cup sugar

2 teaspoons vanilla

¼ teaspoon salt

1. Purée all ingredients until smooth.

2. Pour into a freezer-safe dish, and freeze. Stir every 30 minutes for 4 hours.

## PART-TIME TIP

If the ice cream gets too hard to stir, place it in the food processor again. Blend, and then return it to the freezer and continue stirring every 30 minutes.

# Pumpkin Maple Pie

Serves 8

Perfect with a little vanilla soy ice cream. With only 266 calories per serving and not a bit of butter in sight, this dish will give you bragging rights at Thanksgiving. (And by now, you all know how much I like to brag.)

1 (16-ounce) can pumpkin purée

½ cup maple syrup (Grade B)

1 (12-ounce) block silken tofu

¼ cup sugar

1½ teaspoons cinnamon

½ teaspoon ginger powder

½ teaspoon nutmeg

¼ teaspoon ground cloves

½ teaspoon salt

1 Vegan Cookie Pie Crust (I like this one with Chewy Oatmeal Raisin Cookies)

1. Preheat oven to 400°F.

2. Simply combine all ingredients (except pie crust) until well mixed. Pour into pie crust.

3. Bake for 1 hour. Cool before serving. The pie will set as it cools.

# Vegan Cookie Pie Crust

Serves 8

The perfect all-vegan, all-delicious pie crust for any dessert you ever encounter.

25 small vegan cookies (try any cookie recipe from this chapter!)

¼ cup vegan margarine, melted

½ teaspoon vanilla

1. Process cookies in a food processor until ground up.

2. Add the margarine and vanilla slowly.

3. Press into a pie plate, and pour desired filling on top.

# Chocolate Mocha Frosting

Serves 8

You can never have too many frosting recipes. Just like you can never have too much money or look enough like Brad Pitt. Just saying. If you're feeling frisky, pair this with The From Scratch Chocolate Cake (see dinner plan 10 in chapter 13) for something truly decadent.

¼ cup strong black coffee, cooled

⅓ cup vegan margarine

2 teaspoons vanilla

⅓ cup cocoa powder

3 cups powdered sugar

1. Mix the coffee, margarine, and vanilla together in a medium bowl. Make sure it's smooth and uniform. Then add the cocoa powder.

2. Slowly add in the powdered sugar. Add a bit more than 3 cups if needed. Consistency should be rich and smooth.

# Chocolate Mocha Ice Cream

Serves 6

Have a coffee lover (or five) in the family? Woo them with this: vegan ice cream and coffee combined, vegan style. They won't be able to deny you. It's like a magic spell, but it tastes better.

1 cup vegan chocolate chips

1 cup soy or almond milk

1 (12-ounce) block silken tofu

⅓ cup sugar

2 tablespoons instant coffee

2 teaspoons vanilla

¼ teaspoon salt

1. In a small saucepan over very low heat, melt chocolate chips until smooth. Stir often so it doesn't burn onto the pan.

2. In a blender, blend up the soy or almond milk, tofu, sugar, instant coffee, vanilla, and salt. Keep blending until you get a creamy consistency. This might take 2–4 minutes, depending on your blender. Add the melted chips and blend until smooth.

3. Pour mixture into a freezer-proof dish. Place in freezer.

4. Stir every 30 minutes for 4 hours.

# Raspberry Lemon Cupcakes

**Makes 18 cupcakes**

Give these to a sweetheart on Valentine's Day. Or hog them all to yourself if you don't have a valentine. Either way is somehow satisfying.

½ cup vegan margarine, softened

1 cup sugar

½ teaspoon vanilla

¾ cup soy milk

½ teaspoon lemon extract

2 tablespoons lemon juice

Zest from 2 lemons

1¾ cups flour

1½ teaspoons baking powder

½ teaspoon baking soda

¼ teaspoon salt

¾ cup diced raspberries

1. Preheat oven to 350°F. Grease muffin tins with vegan margarine.

2. Beat the margarine and sugar together. Add the vanilla, soy milk, lemon extract, lemon juice, and lemon zest.

3. In a different bowl, sift together the flour, baking powder, baking soda, and salt.

4. Mix the wet and dry ingredients together. Carefully fold in the raspberries.

5. Pour batter so each muffin cup is ¾ full. Bake for about 17 minutes. Lovely!

# Chocolate Peanut Butter Explosion Pie

Serves 8

It may not be healthy, but it is delicious. It also has the word *explosion* in the title. Honestly, who cares about a little excess every once in a while? Chocolate and Peanut Butter is like the Romeo and Juliet of the food world. And after all, isn't it time you were a little more romantic?

¾ cup vegan chocolate chips

1 (12-ounce) block silken tofu

½ cup peanut butter plus ¾ cup

2 tablespoons soy milk plus ½ cup

1 Vegan Cookie Pie Crust (see recipe earlier in this chapter)

2–2½ cups powdered sugar

Rice or soy whipped cream (optional, but I suggest splurging a little!)

1. Melt the chocolate chips in a saucepan over very low heat.

2. Purée the tofu, ½ cup peanut butter, and 2 tablespoons soy milk. Add the melted chocolate chips. Continue blending until everything is smooth.

3. Pour mixture into pie crust and chill for 1 hour.

4. In a medium saucepan on low heat, melt the ¾ cup peanut butter, ½ cup soy milk, and powdered sugar. You may need a bit more soy milk to make everything a smooth consistency.

5. Spread the mixture over the top of the cooled pie and return to the fridge to chill for another 30 minutes or until firm. Serve with whipped "cream" if desired.

# Chewy Oatmeal Raisin Cookies

**Makes 18 dozen cookies**

Who on this earth doesn't like oatmeal raisin cookies? Eat them with a tall glass of almond milk. Leave them out for old St. Nick, or keep them all to yourself. (He gets enough cookies, come to think of it.)

⅓ cup vegan margarine, softened

½ cup brown sugar

¼ cup sugar

⅓ cup applesauce

1 teaspoon vanilla

2 tablespoons soy milk

¾ cup whole wheat flour

½ teaspoon baking soda

½ teaspoon cinnamon

½ teaspoon ground ginger

1¾ cups quick-cooking oats

⅔ cup raisins

1. Preheat oven to 350°F.

2. Mix margarine and sugars until smooth. Add the applesauce, vanilla, and soy milk. Combine well.

3. Sift the flour, baking soda, cinnamon, and ginger together in a bowl. Then, combine the wet and dry mixtures.

4. Stir in the oats and raisins last.

5. Drop round balls of dough onto a greased cookie sheet and bake for 12 minutes.

# Very Berry Banana Cookies

**Makes about 1 dozen cookies**

A sweet and unfamiliar treat. The combination of blueberry preserves, dried blueberries, cranberries, and the pinch of cinnamon will have you smacking you lips and coming back for seconds—and thirds.

1¾ cups whole wheat flour

1 teaspoon baking powder

¼ teaspoon salt

¼ teaspoon cinnamon

½ cup blueberry preserves

½ cup almond milk

¾ cup rolled oats

1 medium banana

½ cup dried cranberries

¼ cup dried blueberries

Raw almonds for topping

1. Preheat oven to 350°F.

2. Combine the flour, baking powder, salt, cinnamon, preserves, and almond milk in a bowl. Mix well.

3. Mix the oats in. Add the banana into the batter by mashing it up with a fork.

4. Fold in the dried cranberries and blueberries.

5. Roll into 1½" balls and place them on a well-greased cookie sheet. Press an almond into the center of each little cookie. Cook for about 22 minutes. Keep checking on them to make certain the bottoms don't burn and the middles aren't mushy!

# Easy Blackberry Cornbread

**Makes about 1 dozen pieces**

This cornbread is perfect if you don't enjoy the overly saccharine heaviness of some cornbread recipes. The sweetness comes entirely from the fresh, ripe blackberries. The dark juice bleeds into the corn, and is Just. Plain. Delicious.

1¾ cups cornmeal

1 teaspoon baking powder

½ cup almond milk

1 (6-ounce) serving vanilla soy yogurt

½ (15-ounce) can corn, or 1 (8-ounce) bag frozen corn, thawed

1 teaspoon honey

2 pints fresh blackberries

1. Preheat oven to 350°F.

2. Mix the cornmeal, baking powder, almond milk, and soy yogurt until everything sticks together.

3. Fold in the corn and honey.

4. Gently fold 1½ pints of blackberries, taking care not to break them.

5. Press mixture into greased baking dish and press remaining blackberries into the top of the batter. Cook for about 30 minutes.

# Perfect Pumpkin Bread

Serves 6

Whenever I have a massive craving for something I can eat all day long as a breakfast, snack, or dessert, I think of making a loaf of sweetened bread. This pumpkin bread is fast, simple, and infused with the homey flavors of autumn. Eat it with jam for breakfast, vegan margarine as a snack or side, or underneath some soy vanilla ice cream for a dessert!

1¾ cups whole wheat flour

⅔ can packed pumpkin

1 (6-ounce) container vanilla soy yogurt

½ cup oats

¼ cup almond milk

1 teaspoon honey

¾ teaspoon cinnamon

½ teaspoon nutmeg

¼ cup walnuts

¼ cup oats for topping

1. Preheat oven to 400°F.

2. In a large bowl, combine flour with pumpkin, soy yogurt and oats. Mix well to form a dough.

3. Add almond milk and continue mixing.

4. Fold in honey, cinnamon, and nutmeg.

5. Grease a pan with vegan margarine. Roll dough into a loaf shape. Top with oats and walnuts. Cook for 40 minutes, checking the bottom of the bread to make sure it's browned but not burnt!

# Vegan Chocolate-Coconut Ice Cream

**Makes about 1½ pints**

Almost all non-vegan recipes can be turned vegan by simply substituting the fat (usually milk, butter) with another vegan fat (nuts). This frequently yields absolutely incredible results that are—dare we say—better than the originals.

1 cup packaged or fresh, shredded coconut

1 cup cashews

1 cup pecans

1¾ cups water

2½ teaspoons vanilla

1 cup maple syrup (Grade B has the fullest, richest flavor)

¼ cup dark cocoa powder

¼ teaspoon ground coffee

1. If you have the time, patience, and coordination, shuck a fresh coconut and process it using the grate tool on your processor. This provides the most scrumptious and mouthwatering shredded coconut imaginable. Use packaged otherwise.

2. Put all ingredients, except the shredded coconut, into the food processor and blend until smooth. Then add shredded coconut and pulse a few times.

3. If you don't have an ice cream maker (and let's be honest, who has an ice cream maker?) just pop this puppy into a plastic container, cover, and stick in the freezer overnight.

# Death by Raw Chocolate Vegan "Cheese"Cake

Serves 12

Are you looking for the perfect dish to convince your skeptical friends that you haven't completely gone off the deep end with all this vegan malarkey? You have come to the right place! When we say "cheese"cake we do truly mean, this *tastes* like cheesecake. We mean, watch out, because you should be arrested for assault and battery, as this dish is going to knock your Part-Time Vegan-doubting friends out.

**To Make Crust:**

½ cup pecans

½ cup walnuts

2 tablespoons cacao nibs

2–3 tablespoons agave nectar

Dash salt

**To Make Filling:**

½ cup coconut oil

3½ cups raw cashews (soaked 1–4 hours ahead of time)

4 dates

¾ cup agave nectar (amber, if you can find it)

½ cup maple syrup (Grade B, if you can find it)

½ teaspoon ground coffee

½ cup water

2 teaspoons vanilla

½ cup cocoa powder

½ cup dark cocoa powder (Hershey's works great)

Dash salt

1 small (5-ounce) bag of pretzels, crushed

**To Make Crust:**

1. Blend all ingredients for the crust in the food processor. You want the crust to have a "choppy" look to it, so don't blend too much.

2. Press the crust mixture into a 9" pie plate, covering the entire surface area.

**To Make Filling:**

1. Melt coconut oil by placing it into a plastic bag, and setting the bag into a small bowl of hot water. It needs to be liquefied for this recipe to work.

2. Combine all of the ingredients for the filling (including the liquefied coconut oil) in the processor and blend for a good few minutes. The texture should be creamy, the taste dense and rich.

3. Spoon the filling mixture out onto the crust. Then top with crumbled pretzels of your choice, and stick in the freezer for two hours to let the cheesecake "set." It will NOT freeze, don't worry.

4. Allow to defrost in the fridge for 30 minutes before serving. After defrosting, the "cheese"cake may be stored, covered by aluminum foil, in the fridge for up to a week.

# Lemon Poppy Chewy Cake with Blueberry Drizzle

**Serves 12**

This colorful, fragrant recipe will make lemon-lovers go gaga. It's a great summertime cake that has a unique and dense texture. I like to decorate the top with whole blueberries and impress my friends. What can I say? A couple well-placed blueberries and you're in.

3 cups whole wheat flour

1 teaspoon baking soda

1 teaspoon baking powder

½ teaspoon salt

3½ teaspoons poppy seeds

2 teaspoons vanilla

⅓ cup lemon juice

1 cup apple juice

⅔ cup maple syrup (Grade B, if possible)

Rind of 3 lemons

½ to 1 pint of fresh blueberries

**To Make Blueberry Drizzle**

½ cup fresh blueberries

½ cup vegan margarine

3 cups powdered sugar

1 tablespoon lemon juice

½ teaspoon strawberry extract (look for this near the vanilla extract in the baking section of your market)

½ teaspoon apple cider vinegar

1. Preheat oven to 350°F.

2. Mix the flour, baking soda, baking powder, salt, and poppy seeds together.

3. Add the vanilla, lemon juice, apple juice, and maple syrup.

4. Take the food processor and use the grating tool (or you can do it by hand) to grate the rinds of 3 lemons. Add the lemon rinds to the batter.

5. Grease a 9" pie plate with vegan butter. Don't forget that part! Fill with batter.

6. Bake 30–35 minutes.

7. Wait until cake is completely cool before drizzling with blueberry icing and topping with fresh blueberries.

**To Make Blueberry Drizzle**
1. Simply combine all ingredients in a food processor and drizzle on top of cooled cake.

## PART-TIME TIP

Aside from adding apple cider vinegar to a lot of vegan recipes to curd almond or soy milk, I often use to it give a kick to recipes that usually call for cheese. Adding it to this frosting creates an almost "cream cheesy" flavor! Fascinating, I know.

# Raw to Die for Apple Pie with Berry Topping

**FIBER**

Serves 12

I lived somewhere for a little while where apple pie was the ugly stepsister to key lime pie. Needless to say, I felt the need to defend the maligned apple pie, and thus set out to make my own version every autumn. This here apple pie is free of butter and refined sugar, and you'll love yourself for eating it. No more regret after dessert!

A word of warning: This pie is best made and eaten on the same day; otherwise, the natural juices of the apples will make the crust soggy!

**To Make Crust**

½ cup dried cranberries

2 cups pecans

½ cup walnuts

½ cup dates

**To Make Filling**

6 medium Gala apples, peeled and cored

2 teaspoons honey

2 teaspoons cinnamon

½ cup raisins

½ cup rolled oats

¾ cup dates

**To Make Berry Topping**

¾ cup dried cranberries

2 large squirts of honey

2 handfuls red grapes

¾ cup water

1 handful of blueberries

**To Make Crust**

1. Process all the ingredients for the crust in the food processor. Press it into the bottom of a 9" pie plate.

**To Make Filling**

1. Peel and core the apples. Yep, this will get tedious. Dice them when you're finished.

2. Add ½ of the diced apples into the processor and process them. If you do more than this, you may overwhelm the machine and you could have a landmine situation on your hands.

3. Add the honey, cinnamon, and raisins to the apple mixture and process together. Dump this mixture into a bowl.

4. Process the remaining apples, and then process both apple mixtures together. Add the oats and dates, and process for another 2 minutes.

5. Spoon the apple mixture into the crust. Garnish with raisins if you want to be a Superman. Set in the freezer for an hour or so.

**To Make Berry Topping**

1. Process all of the Berry Sauce Topping ingredients together. Set aside in the fridge until serving time. Dollop on top of pie when ready to serve. Yummmm!

# Resources

Some stores, brands, and websites that will help you on your vegan journey.

**Bob's Red Mill** *www.bobsredmill.com*
Bob's Red Mill is another excellent resource for finding vegan cooking ingredients including: TVP, egg-replacer, white whole wheat flour, and vital wheat gluten.

**Whole Foods** *www.wholefoodsmarket.com*
Whole foods is a vegan-friendly supermarket chain that is a veritable treasure trove of important vegan ingredients including: vital wheat gluten, seitan, vegan margarine, nutritional yeast, vegan cheese, almond milk, carob chips and more. Some Whole Foods stores even have ready-to-eat take out vegan items like vegan egg salad, or vegan buttercream in the bakery!

**The Vegan Store** *www.veganstore.com*
A veritable clearinghouse of all things vegan, this site also has lots of food options you can order, including vegan marshmallows!

**The Post-Punk Kitchen** *www.theppk.com*
The "PPK" is an amazing online resource for vegan bakers. Full of helpful tips, recipes, and an online forum, any and all of your vegan baking queries can be answered at this friendly, upbeat, albeit young-skewing website.

**Food Fight Grocery** *www.foodfightgrocery.com*
Another amazing online grocery that provides entertainment with it's hilarious attitude, as well as every vegan junk food in the book.

**Vegan Yum Yum Blog** *http://veganyumyum.com*
Once you're ready to take your vegan training wheels off and venture into more gourmet options, or if you just want to enjoy some great vegan food porn pics, check out this YUM yum blog!

# Index

# About the Author

Cherise Grifoni is a Part-Time Vegan. A full-blown vegetarian for seven years, she recently converted to veganism after she discovered that cheese products were a major factor in her migraine headache attacks. And even though she has always avoided milk and eggs, who can resist the temptation of a cupcake from one of New York City's famed bakeries every now and again? Certainly not her.

As the blogger at Your Vegan Zombie (*www.yourveganzombie .blogspot.com*) and the president of an impromptu unofficial Vegan Cooking Club while a student at New York University, she has always strived to present veganism as something easy and doable.

Cherise's approach to veganism is humorous and casual, which she hopes displays veganism as less of a mystery and more of an approach-able, feel-good step you can take on the path to looking and feeling better. She believes veganism shouldn't be about guilt and deprivation, but about creating new, spectacular, simple foods that will have you wondering why you never tried this in the first place!

# the hungry
# editor

# Foodies Unite!

Bring your appetite and follow The Hungry Editor who really loves to eat. She'll be discussing (and drooling over) all things low-fat and full-fat, local and fresh, canned and frozen, highbrow and lowbrow...

When it comes to good eats, The Hungry Editor (and her tastebuds) do not discriminate!

It's a Feeding Frenzy—dig in!

Sign up for our newsletter at

## www.adamsmedia.com/blog/cooking

and download our free **Top Ten Gourmet Meals for $7** recipes!